DEVOPS INTERVIEW ACCELERATOR: 8 REAL LABS, 100+ REALTIME INTERVIEW QUESTIONS ASKED

First edition. October 12, 2025.

ISBN: 979-8232059378

Written by Yash d..

Table of Contents

How Hiring Teams Really Score DevOps Candidates 1

Interview Mindset: From Nervous to Interview-Ready 12

Lab Framework: Run, Record, Reflect (8 Real Labs Overview) 24

Lab 1 — Linux & Troubleshooting: Live Crash and Fix 38

Lab 2 — CI/CD Pipeline Rescue: Fix a Failing Build Under Pressure 51

Lab 3 — Infrastructure as Code: Safe Terraform Change & Rollback 64

Lab 4 — Kubernetes: Debug a Canary Deployment 72

Lab 5 — Observability & SLOs: Show Me You Can Measure Reliability 84

Lab 6 — Performance Triage: Small Load Test, Big Insights 95

Lab 7 — Security & Compliance: Quick Audit and Fix Plan 106

100+ Real-Time Interview Questions (With BUILD-Style Model Answers) 119

System Design for DevOps Interviews: Quick Blueprints Recruiters Love . 146

Answering Behavioral & Leadership Questions for QA/SRE Roles 157

Interview Day Toolkit: One-Page Cheat Sheets & 30-Day Practice Plan 169

Appendix A — Companion GitHub Repo & How to Show It in Interviews 181

Appendix B — Template Artifacts (Postmortem, Runbook, Test Plan, CI YAMLs) 192

To every DevOps aspirant who's tired of endless job searches, confusing interview questions, and rejection emails — this book is for you.

To the dreamers who see a career in DevOps not just as a job, but as a journey of continuous growth—this is your compass.

And finally, to those who dare to ask, experiment, fail, and try again—your perseverance is the engine of progress.

Real-Time Interview Preparation
DevOps
Interview
Accelerator
8 REAL LABS, 100+ REALTIME
INTERVIEW QUESTIONS ASKED
Selected
YASH D.

Preface

Entering the world of DevOps can feel like stepping into a high-stakes performance arena. The intersection of development, operations, automation, and system reliability creates a landscape where technical knowledge alone is no longer enough. Recruiters and hiring managers are increasingly looking for professionals who can **demonstrate real-world competence under pressure, solve complex problems quickly, and communicate effectively across teams**. DevOps roles demand a unique blend of analytical thinking, hands-on execution, and the soft skills to navigate collaborative environments. This book, *DevOps Interview Accelerator: 8 Real Labs, 100+ Realtime Interview Questions Asked*, has been crafted to equip you with exactly what it takes to **stand out in these interviews** and walk in prepared, confident, and ready to impress.

Unlike traditional guides that simply list tools, commands, or theoretical explanations, this book is built around **practical immersion**. It assumes that you already know the fundamentals of Linux, scripting, containers, and cloud platforms. Instead of rehashing theory, it thrusts you into **real-world scenarios** designed to simulate the challenges you will face in a live DevOps environment. Each lab, artifact, and exercise mirrors situations that hiring managers deliberately seek to evaluate, providing a clear window into your operational thinking and problem-solving capabilities.

The core philosophy behind this book is simple: **interviews are won by those who can do, demonstrate, and communicate—not just those who can memorize answers**. Many candidates struggle because they focus exclusively on memorizing commands or facts. While this knowledge is essential, it only scratches the surface of what recruiters truly measure. In reality, hiring teams are looking for **how you respond under pressure, how you troubleshoot unexpected failures, and how you reason about complex systems**. They want evidence that you can contribute immediately, adapt to dynamic environments, and apply best practices to real challenges. This book provides a structured path to showcase that ability through a combination of hands-on labs, scenario-based exercises, and clearly defined templates.

One of the key innovations of this book is its **lab-based approach**, which is designed to simulate the fast-paced, problem-solving nature of real DevOps work. Each lab is intentionally crafted to create tension, unpredictability, and real-time decision-making. By working through these labs, you are not just learning commands or pipelines—you are experiencing the **stress and decision-making processes** that mirror high-pressure incidents in production environments. This is exactly the type of practical experience that makes interviewers take notice.

Alongside the hands-on labs, the book integrates **a strategic framework for preparation**. Interviews often evaluate candidates across multiple dimensions: technical depth, troubleshooting ability, system design acumen, automation expertise, observability skills, security awareness, and soft skills including communication and leadership. This book synthesizes these dimensions into a cohesive preparation strategy, offering you tools and exercises to build confidence, reduce anxiety, and systematically reinforce your abilities. You are guided not only in what to practice but also **how to think like a DevOps engineer in an interview setting**, translating real-world scenarios into articulate, structured responses.

Another defining feature of this guide is its **focus on reproducible artifacts**. Modern DevOps interviews increasingly require candidates to provide evidence of their work—whether it's a GitHub repository, a pipeline configuration, a test plan, or a postmortem. This book equips you with templates and guidelines to **document your work professionally**, demonstrating thoughtfulness, thoroughness, and an understanding of industry best practices. Interviewers can see that you don't just execute tasks; you design workflows, anticipate challenges, and create maintainable solutions. By incorporating these artifacts into your preparation, you transform your personal learning into a tangible portfolio of professional capability.

The book also emphasizes **communication and behavioral excellence**, which are often underestimated yet crucial components of success. Being able to explain your approach, justify your decisions, and convey impact in a concise, structured manner can make the difference between a strong candidate and a top performer. Real-time labs and scenario exercises are paired with techniques for articulating your thought process clearly. This dual focus ensures that your technical skill is matched by your ability to **influence, collaborate, and**

lead—qualities that are increasingly valued in DevOps roles where cross-functional interaction is constant.

One of the unique strengths of this book is its attention to **time-bound, realistic practice**. Unlike theoretical guides that span hundreds of pages of information, the labs and exercises are concise, targeted, and designed to fit within realistic preparation schedules. This approach allows you to **measure progress, reflect on outcomes, and iterate quickly**, mirroring the rapid feedback cycles you will encounter in actual DevOps work. You are encouraged not just to complete exercises but to record your process, analyze mistakes, and refine your approach—a methodology that demonstrates maturity and operational awareness in interviews.

The book also includes a **comprehensive repository of real-time interview questions and model answers**. These are not generic or academic-style questions but are curated from real interviews and reflect the types of challenges DevOps candidates face in high-performing companies. Each answer is structured not just to provide a correct response, but to **illustrate problem-solving methodology, reasoning, and best practices**. By studying these examples, you can internalize not only what to answer but also **how to answer effectively**, increasing your ability to impress interviewers under pressure.

In addition, this guide addresses the often-overlooked **system design component of DevOps interviews**. System design is no longer reserved for software engineers alone; SREs, QA automation engineers, and DevOps practitioners are now routinely asked to design scalable, resilient, and observable systems. This book equips you with **quick blueprints and practical templates**, enabling you to articulate design choices clearly and convincingly. You are taught to think in terms of **modularity, fault tolerance, scalability, and maintainability**, ensuring that your responses demonstrate both technical depth and strategic insight.

Finally, preparation without execution is incomplete. This book provides a **practical 30-day practice plan, cheat sheets, and structured guidance** to ensure that your study time translates into tangible results. It emphasizes active learning, scenario-based drills, artifact creation, and progressive complexity—mirroring the iterative approach that effective DevOps teams use to improve services. By following this regimen, you can **transform nervousness into confidence, uncertainty into clarity, and preparation into performance.**

In summary, *DevOps Interview Accelerator: 8 Real Labs, 100+ Realtime Interview Questions Asked* is more than a guide; it is a **preparation ecosystem.** It combines hands-on labs, realistic scenarios, templates for documentation, behavioral and leadership guidance, and curated interview questions to deliver a holistic preparation experience. Candidates who engage deeply with this book will not only gain technical competence but also **develop the operational mindset, communication skills, and problem-solving confidence** that differentiate outstanding candidates in competitive DevOps interviews.

This book is ideal for anyone seeking to **bridge the gap between knowledge and execution**. Whether you are preparing for your first DevOps interview, transitioning from QA or traditional operations, or aiming to secure a senior SRE position, this book provides the practical insights, tools, and structured practice necessary to succeed. It is designed to **make you think, act, and present like a seasoned professional**, increasing your chances of performing well under the intense scrutiny of modern DevOps interviews.

By the time you finish this book, you will not only be able to answer questions but also **demonstrate competence in real-world labs, showcase polished artifacts, and convey confidence and clarity in your responses**. This combination of skills, evidence, and presentation is precisely what recruiters and hiring managers are seeking in top-tier DevOps candidates.

The journey this book offers is intense, practical, and designed for **results-oriented preparation**. For candidates who commit to working through the exercises, reflecting on outcomes, and mastering the artifacts, it promises a transformation from nervousness and uncertainty to readiness and confidence. By the end, you will not just be prepared—you will be **interview-ready, performance-ready, and ready to showcase the DevOps expertise that recruiters value most**.

How Hiring Teams Really Score DevOps Candidates

Understanding the Mindset of Hiring Teams

DevOps interviews are not about trick questions or theoretical buzzwords. They are about discovering how a candidate thinks, collaborates, and delivers under real operational pressures. Most companies hiring DevOps professionals are not just looking for people who know tools like Docker, Jenkins, Kubernetes, or Terraform. They are evaluating whether the person can apply those tools to create scalable, reliable, and automated delivery systems that serve real business needs.

Hiring managers and technical panels often approach interviews with one key question in mind: *Can this candidate handle real-world production challenges and contribute effectively to cross-functional delivery?* Every round of a DevOps interview—technical screening, practical tests, or final discussions—revolves around that question.

Freshers are usually evaluated on their conceptual understanding and learning potential, while experienced professionals are assessed based on real implementation experience and troubleshooting depth. Regardless of experience level, hiring teams focus on **clarity, collaboration, and context awareness**—three critical aspects that define strong DevOps professionals.

What Hiring Managers Look for Beyond Tool Knowledge

Technical Versatility

A common misconception among candidates is that DevOps success depends on mastering specific tools. While tool proficiency is valuable, recruiters prioritize versatility over tool obsession. They want candidates who can adapt to changing technologies and integrate new solutions efficiently.

For example, if an interviewer asks, "How do you manage CI/CD pipelines?" they are not just expecting a description of Jenkins pipelines. They want to know if you understand the **concept of continuous integration**, **artifact management**, **deployment strategies**, and **rollback mechanisms**—knowledge that can be applied across Jenkins, GitLab CI, or GitHub Actions.

Hiring teams score candidates higher when they demonstrate an understanding of **principles**, not just **processes.**

Problem-Solving and Production Thinking

The best DevOps engineers think like firefighters and architects at the same time. Interviewers often present a scenario such as:

Scenario:

"You notice that one of the microservices in production is throwing 5xx errors intermittently. Monitoring dashboards show CPU spikes in the Kubernetes cluster. How would you approach troubleshooting this issue?"

A strong candidate would respond by first clarifying the problem's scope, then outlining a methodical approach:

- Check pod logs and identify error patterns.
- Verify resource allocation and autoscaling configurations.
- Examine the cluster's node utilization and network bottlenecks.
- Review recent deployments and image versions.

Hiring teams score such answers highly because they show structured thinking and situational control rather than a random list of commands.

Communication and Collaboration

DevOps is a collaborative discipline that connects development and operations. Interviewers often assess communication skills subtly through behavioral questions. A simple question like, "Describe a time when you handled a failed deployment," reveals whether the candidate blames others or focuses on solutions.

Strong candidates say things like, "We identified that our staging environment lacked parity with production, so we implemented automated environment provisioning using Terraform to ensure consistency." This reflects accountability and teamwork—traits every hiring manager values.

How Interviews Are Structured for DevOps Roles

Most companies follow a structured, multi-stage evaluation pattern to assess both technical competence and cultural fit. Understanding this structure can help candidates prepare more strategically.

Stage 1: Screening and Conceptual Validation

The first round often includes a recruiter or a junior DevOps engineer who checks the candidate's familiarity with core DevOps principles.

Typical questions include:

- What is the difference between continuous integration and continuous deployment?
- How do you handle version control branching strategies in a collaborative team?
- What monitoring tools have you used and why?

Freshers are expected to show conceptual clarity, while experienced candidates are expected to connect their answers to real-world systems.

Stage 2: Hands-On Technical Assessment

This is where most candidates are filtered out. Practical labs or take-home tests are designed to simulate production challenges. Tasks may include:

- Writing a Dockerfile and optimizing image size.
- Creating a Jenkins pipeline that builds and deploys a sample application.
- Setting up Terraform infrastructure for a simple web application.
- Diagnosing a failing Kubernetes pod and explaining the fix.

Recruiters often score these assessments based on reproducibility, clarity, and error handling. Candidates who document their steps, comment on their code, and follow logical structures score higher than those who rush through commands.

Stage 3: System Design and Real-Time Scenario Discussion

This round is usually conducted by senior DevOps engineers or solution architects. The focus shifts from "how you do it" to "why you do it."

Example scenario:

"You need to design a CI/CD pipeline for a microservices-based e-commerce application deployed on AWS EKS. How would you structure it?"

The hiring team evaluates:

- Understanding of source control integration (Git branching, triggers)
- Pipeline stages (build, test, deploy)
- Infrastructure as Code usage
- Secrets management (AWS Secrets Manager, HashiCorp Vault)

- Deployment strategy (blue-green, canary)
- Rollback and monitoring mechanisms

Strong answers balance **technical depth** with **clarity and prioritization**, showing that the candidate can think strategically while implementing practically.

Stage 4: Behavioral and Cultural Fit Round

Many candidates underestimate this stage. However, hiring teams know that a great DevOps culture depends on collaboration and communication. Expect questions like:

- How do you handle conflicts between developers and operations teams?
- How do you prioritize issues during an outage?
- Describe how you keep yourself updated with new DevOps trends.

Experienced recruiters listen for maturity, composure, and adaptability rather than textbook answers.

The Scoring Framework Behind the Scenes

Every organization uses its own evaluation matrix, but most follow a weighted scoring model. Understanding this helps candidates align their preparation to the areas that matter most.

Core Competency Areas

1. Technical Foundation (30–40%)

Includes understanding of Linux, networking, containers, scripting, and CI/CD workflows. Candidates should show practical comfort with command-line operations and configuration management.

2. Problem-Solving and Debugging (20–25%)

Hiring teams often test this through live troubleshooting sessions. Candidates who narrate their thought process while solving problems often score higher.

3. Automation and Infrastructure as Code (15–20%)

Evaluates knowledge of tools like Terraform, Ansible, or CloudFormation. Recruiters look for reproducible automation practices and clarity in environment provisioning.

4. Cloud and Deployment Strategy (15–20%)

Covers cloud-native design, security policies, scaling, and cost optimization.

5. Collaboration and Culture Fit (10–15%)

Assesses soft skills, accountability, and DevOps mindset—especially for leadership or cross-team roles.

Hiring panels usually share feedback internally, scoring candidates on these five axes. A balanced performer in all categories often ranks higher than someone extremely strong in one but weak in others.

Real Interview Scenarios and Evaluation Insights

Scenario 1: Debugging a Failed Deployment

Question:

"Your Jenkins pipeline fails during the deployment stage with a timeout error. How would you troubleshoot?"

What Interviewers Look For:

They want to see if the candidate can isolate the failure point logically. A structured answer might include:

- Checking Jenkins console logs for specific stage failures.
- Verifying network connectivity between Jenkins agents and the deployment environment.
- Reviewing credential validity and target host accessibility.
- Ensuring that deployment scripts handle rollback conditions gracefully.

A well-organized response demonstrates composure and technical control.

Scenario 2: Designing Resilient Infrastructure

Question:

"Your application experiences traffic surges during festive sales. How do you ensure uptime and scalability?"

Strong Answer Indicators:

- Implementing auto-scaling groups in cloud environments.
- Using load balancers and caching layers.
- Designing stateless application tiers.
- Applying infrastructure as code to scale infrastructure predictably.
- Adding observability tools like Prometheus and Grafana.

Candidates who connect each technical choice to business impact—such as minimizing downtime or optimizing cost—stand out clearly to interviewers.

Scenario 3: Managing Secrets and Configurations

Question:

"How would you manage sensitive credentials in your CI/CD pipelines?"

Good Responses Include:

- Storing secrets in tools like HashiCorp Vault, AWS Secrets Manager, or Kubernetes Secrets.
- Ensuring no credentials are hardcoded in repositories.
- Using environment variables securely and rotating keys periodically.

Recruiters score high for candidates who balance security best practices with operational practicality.

The Psychology of DevOps Interviews

What Interviewers Are Really Thinking

While candidates focus on correctness, interviewers often focus on *approach*. They want to know:

- How you think under pressure.
- Whether you can explain complex setups in simple terms.
- How quickly you adapt to new problems.

A technically perfect but uncommunicative candidate often scores lower than someone slightly less skilled but more collaborative and composed. DevOps roles sit at the intersection of multiple teams, so adaptability and empathy play a big role in hiring decisions.

The "Teach-Back" Factor

Some hiring managers use a technique called "teach-back"—they ask you to explain a concept as if you were teaching it to a junior engineer. This reveals both depth of understanding and communication skills. For example:

"Explain the CI/CD pipeline concept to a non-technical project manager."

Candidates who respond with simple, logical narratives like, "CI/CD automates the process of integrating code, testing it, and deploying it, so that changes reach production faster and with fewer errors," tend to score higher than those who recite technical jargon.

Common Mistakes Candidates Make

Overemphasis on Tools

Many candidates prepare a long list of tools but fail to connect them to practical use cases. Interviewers lose interest when answers sound memorized rather than experience-driven.

Ignoring Soft Skills

DevOps success depends on cross-team collaboration. Candidates who fail to show empathy, documentation habits, or ownership during incident discussions often receive lower scores.

Lack of Scenario Preparedness

Hiring teams appreciate candidates who can discuss their past incidents or simulated projects. Even freshers can demonstrate initiative by describing lab setups or GitHub projects that mimic real DevOps workflows.

Failing to Explain Trade-offs

When discussing infrastructure choices, strong candidates explain why they chose one tool or pattern over another. Saying "I used Kubernetes because it scales well and offers rolling updates" is better than "I used Kubernetes because everyone does."

How to Position Yourself for Higher Scores

Practice Storytelling Through Scenarios

Interviewers remember stories more than scripts. Frame your answers around problem, approach, and outcome. For example:

- "Our deployment pipeline took 30 minutes, so I optimized build caching and reduced it to 8 minutes."
- "We faced configuration drift issues, so I implemented Terraform for consistent provisioning."

Such concise, impact-driven examples make a strong impression.

Build and Showcase Real Labs

Candidates who can show working repositories or lab setups during interviews demonstrate genuine skill. Even simple projects—like automating Nginx deployment using Ansible or setting up CI/CD for a sample Python app—show initiative and depth.

Prepare for Behavioral Scenarios

Instead of generic answers, reflect on your teamwork and problem-solving examples. For instance:

"When production went down, I helped coordinate between developers and the SRE team, created a temporary rollback, and added post-incident monitoring to prevent recurrence."

Hiring teams notice candidates who combine technical and interpersonal maturity.

Final Thoughts: What Hiring Teams Ultimately Seek

DevOps hiring is about mindset alignment, not memorization. Teams look for individuals who:

- Think in systems, not silos.
- Automate with intent, not habit.
- Communicate with clarity.
- Learn continuously from both success and failure.

The strongest DevOps candidates are those who can describe complex systems simply, recover from failures confidently, and adapt rapidly to changing environments. Whether you are a fresher learning pipelines or an experienced engineer designing hybrid infrastructures, your success depends on showing curiosity, ownership, and collaboration in every conversation.

If you can make an interviewer believe that you not only know *how* DevOps works but also *why* it matters, you will not just pass interviews—you will accelerate your DevOps career.

Interview Mindset: From Nervous to Interview-Ready

Understanding the Role of Mindset in DevOps Interviews

A DevOps interview is not only a test of your technical knowledge—it is a window into how you think, communicate, and operate under uncertainty. Every hiring manager knows that the best engineers are not just those who know tools like Docker or Jenkins, but those who can stay calm when production pipelines break at 3 AM, collaborate across teams, and deliver solutions efficiently.

Your mindset, therefore, becomes a decisive factor in interviews. Candidates with a clear, calm, and structured mindset stand out even if their answers are not perfect. Nervous candidates, on the other hand, often underperform despite having strong technical skills. The purpose of this chapter is to help you transition from nervousness to interview readiness, by understanding what interviewers expect, and how to show your competence confidently.

Why Mindset Matters More Than Memorization

Many candidates prepare for DevOps interviews by memorizing commands, definitions, or buzzwords. They forget that interviews are dynamic conversations, not multiple-choice tests. Real hiring panels focus on your thought process—how you break down a problem, how you explain technical concepts, and how you respond when faced with an unfamiliar question.

A strong mindset helps you stay grounded, structured, and logical even when you don't immediately know the answer. Interviewers observe your confidence, composure, and clarity more than your ability to recall syntax. In other words, the way you think is often more important than what you know.

Imagine two candidates in the same interview:

- Candidate A answers every question with exact command-line syntax but fails to explain why that command works.

- Candidate B explains the reasoning, mentions trade-offs, and admits when unsure, but connects the dots logically.

Hiring teams almost always select Candidate B. They want someone who can grow with the system, not just repeat commands.

How Nervousness Affects Performance

The Technical Brain vs. the Emotional Brain

During an interview, your technical brain needs to be active—analyzing, explaining, and structuring information. But when nervousness takes over, the emotional brain interferes, leading to rushed answers, blank moments, and reduced clarity.

Understanding this mechanism helps you control it. Nervousness is a physiological reaction triggered by uncertainty and perceived threat. The interview environment—strangers evaluating you, the risk of rejection—amplifies that threat. However, DevOps interviews reward calm analysis over quick reactions. You need to train yourself to channel the same focus you use during production incidents into your interviews.

Common Symptoms of Interview Nervousness

- Forgetting familiar commands or tools during questioning

- Speaking too fast or too softly

- Overexplaining or jumping between unrelated points

- Getting defensive when corrected

- Losing track of the question midway

Recognizing these patterns early helps you correct them through practice and reflection.

Developing an Interview-Ready Mindset

Step 1: Understand What the Interviewer Wants

Every interviewer has one goal—to find someone reliable, adaptable, and technically capable. The technical questions are simply the medium to test these qualities. Once you realize this, your anxiety begins to fade. You are not being interrogated; you are being evaluated as a potential team member.

Think from the interviewer's side. When they ask, "How do you troubleshoot a failed build in Jenkins?" they are not looking for a perfect step-by-step recipe. They want to see:

- How you approach problems logically
- How you communicate under pressure
- Whether you can prioritize effectively

If you treat every question as a collaborative discussion instead of a test, your tone naturally becomes more confident and your answers more coherent.

Step 2: Shift from Fear to Curiosity

Nervousness is fear-based, curiosity is growth-based. During interviews, replace thoughts like "What if I fail?" with "What can I learn from this conversation?"

Curiosity turns interviews into opportunities. If you don't know an answer, instead of panicking, show interest:

"That's interesting—I haven't implemented that specific configuration, but I've worked with a similar pattern in GitLab CI. I believe the principle would be similar."

This shows confidence, learning agility, and a healthy DevOps mindset.

Step 3: Prepare Through Real Practice

Confidence comes from familiarity. The more you rehearse realistic interview environments, the more your brain adapts.

You can:

- Simulate mock interviews with peers using common DevOps scenarios.
- Explain your daily automation tasks aloud, as if you were teaching them.
- Practice whiteboarding pipeline designs or infrastructure flow.
- Record yourself explaining concepts to identify filler words or unclear phrasing.

This kind of practice develops "muscle memory" for interviews—so when questions come, your mind retrieves structured explanations naturally.

Building Confidence Through Realistic Scenarios

Example 1: The CI/CD Debugging Question

Imagine you are asked: "Your CI/CD pipeline fails at the test stage after a recent commit. How would you identify the issue?"

A nervous candidate might panic and start listing tools randomly: "I'll check Jenkins logs, maybe rerun the build, check dependencies..."

A confident candidate would structure their response:

- Clarify the scope of failure: "I'd first confirm whether the failure is in the build or test phase."

- Analyze the latest changes: "Then I'd review the recent commits to identify what might have affected test configurations."

- Use logs strategically: "Next, I'd check the Jenkins console output and unit test reports to pinpoint the exact failing module."

- Validate dependencies: "If dependencies changed, I'd verify version compatibility in the build file."

This calm structure reflects confidence. Even if the candidate misses a few details, the approach earns high marks.

Example 2: The Kubernetes Troubleshooting Question

Question: "A pod in your Kubernetes cluster keeps restarting. How would you investigate the issue?"

A nervous candidate might rush into: "I'll restart the pod or redeploy the YAML."

A confident candidate explains:

- "I'd start with 'kubectl describe pod' to inspect recent events."

- "Then, I'd review container logs for crash loops."

- "If it's an OOM error, I'd analyze resource requests and limits."

- "I'd also check for liveness probe configurations."

The difference is composure and clarity—products of an interview-ready mindset.

Structuring Your Thoughts During Interviews

The Three-Part Response Framework

Every strong DevOps answer can follow a simple three-step structure:

1. **Context** – Briefly define the problem or principle being discussed.
2. **Approach** – Explain how you would handle or implement it.
3. **Outcome** – Describe the expected or achieved result.

For example:

Question: "What is your approach to infrastructure as code?"

Answer: "Infrastructure as Code means managing environments through versioned scripts rather than manual setups. I use Terraform for provisioning AWS resources because it ensures consistency across environments. Using version control, I can roll back changes easily and maintain traceability."

This structure keeps your answer concise, logical, and confidence-driven.

Managing Anxiety During the Actual Interview

Control Your Breathing and Pace

One of the simplest yet most powerful ways to handle nervousness is controlled breathing. Before or during the interview, take a slow, deep breath. It signals your brain that you're safe, helping you regain composure.

Speak slightly slower than usual. Fast speech often signals nervousness and leads to unclear explanations. A steady pace gives you time to think and your interviewer time to process your response.

Listen Before You Answer

Nervous candidates often interrupt or answer prematurely. Strong candidates listen fully, pause for two seconds, and then respond. That short pause reflects confidence and thoughtfulness.

In scenario-based questions, repeating or paraphrasing the problem also buys you time and shows active listening. For example:

"Just to confirm, you're asking how I'd handle a failed deployment to staging, correct?"

This simple step can make you appear significantly more composed.

Handle Unknown Questions Gracefully

Even top engineers encounter questions they cannot answer immediately. The difference lies in response style.

Bad response: "I'm not sure."

Better response: "I haven't configured that exact tool, but I understand the underlying principle. I'd approach it by reviewing the documentation and replicating it in a test environment."

Such statements show analytical confidence rather than uncertainty.

The Role of Real-World Experience in Confidence

Building Personal Labs

Confidence grows when your learning is experience-based. Setting up your own DevOps lab—even a small one—gives you stories and evidence to support your answers.

For instance:

- Automate an Nginx deployment using Ansible and explain the logic behind your playbook.
- Deploy a simple web app using Docker Compose and highlight how you managed networking between containers.
- Configure a CI/CD pipeline for a demo project on GitHub Actions and note how you handled failures.

When you mention personal implementations, you shift from theoretical answers to experiential storytelling. Interviewers perceive this as authentic confidence.

Learning from Real Incidents

If you've worked in production environments, reflect on your incident-handling experiences. Describe what went wrong, how you diagnosed it, and what preventive measures you added later.

For example:

"We once faced high latency in our microservices. I used Grafana metrics to trace the issue to an inefficient database query. We added caching at the API gateway and reduced latency by 40%."

Such examples demonstrate technical depth and ownership—traits hiring teams value highly.

Transforming Nervous Energy into Productive Focus

The Power of Pre-Interview Rituals

Establishing a routine before interviews conditions your brain for calm focus. Examples include:

- Reviewing three recent projects or labs you've built.
- Reading your notes on CI/CD and infrastructure troubleshooting.
- Taking a 10-minute quiet walk before the call.
- Visualizing a successful, confident interview.

These small rituals help anchor your focus and convert nervous energy into readiness.

Managing Last-Minute Panic

If you feel anxious minutes before the interview:

- Focus on your breathing.
- Remind yourself that interviews are two-way conversations.
- Keep a short summary sheet of your key projects, achievements, and tool experience.
- Avoid cramming or reading new material right before—it increases cognitive load and tension.

How to Think Like a DevOps Interviewer

Understanding what interviewers are truly evaluating helps you respond strategically.

What They Are Looking For

- A calm, analytical problem-solver
- Someone who can explain technical concepts clearly
- Evidence of real project or lab experience
- Awareness of DevOps culture—automation, collaboration, continuous improvement
- Confidence without arrogance

When you think like an interviewer, you naturally tailor your tone, structure, and examples accordingly.

Example: Handling a Tough Question

Question: "Your production deployment failed at midnight. What would be your first steps?"

An anxious candidate might say: "I'd check logs and restart the service."

A confident, structured answer would be:

"First, I'd communicate with the team to confirm if this is a widespread issue or isolated. Then I'd check monitoring dashboards to identify patterns. If it's a recent deployment, I'd review rollback procedures. Once stabilized, I'd perform a post-incident analysis to identify the root cause and update our CI/CD validation checks."

That kind of response shows leadership, calmness, and technical awareness—precisely what hiring teams reward.

Behavioral Mindset Questions and How to Handle Them

Many DevOps interviews include behavioral rounds. These questions often begin with "Tell me about a time when..." and test your mindset, teamwork, and problem ownership.

Example 1: "Tell me about a time you handled a failed deployment."

Strong approach:

- Describe the problem briefly.
- Explain your immediate steps.
- Emphasize teamwork, communication, and learning outcomes.

Example:

"We faced a failed deployment due to incorrect environment variables. I helped roll back to the last stable version, analyzed the logs, and introduced automated variable validation. This reduced future errors and improved deployment reliability."

Example 2: "How do you handle conflicts with developers or

operations teams?"

Good mindset response:

"I focus on aligning goals. In one case, the dev team wanted faster deployments, while operations prioritized stability. I proposed a canary deployment model, allowing gradual rollouts. It balanced both priorities and improved trust across teams."

Behavioral questions give you the opportunity to demonstrate composure, empathy, and DevOps culture awareness.

Continuous Improvement Mindset

Learning from Every Interview

Even rejections can become valuable lessons. After each interview, reflect on:

- Which questions challenged you?
- Where did your explanations lack clarity?
- What topics appeared repeatedly?

Use this reflection to refine your preparation. Over time, each interview becomes a practice ground that makes you calmer and sharper.

Staying Updated and Confident

DevOps evolves rapidly. Confidence comes from staying current. Dedicate weekly time to:

- Experimenting with new CI/CD features.
- Reading release notes of Kubernetes, Terraform, or Jenkins.
- Following DevOps community discussions and blogs.

When you discuss new trends naturally, interviewers sense enthusiasm and preparedness.

Final Thoughts: Confidence as a DevOps Skill

Confidence is not arrogance or over-assurance—it is calm awareness of your abilities and limitations. The best DevOps professionals are humble learners who can handle unknowns without panic.

When you prepare systematically, practice real scenarios, and view interviews as learning conversations, nervousness fades naturally.

Remember: hiring teams are not looking for perfection; they are looking for reliability, clarity, and growth potential. If you show structured thinking, genuine curiosity, and composure under pressure, you will not just be interview-ready—you will be career-ready.

Your mindset is your most powerful DevOps tool. Use it well, and every interview becomes another deployment step toward success.

Lab Framework: Run, Record, Reflect (8 Real Labs Overview)

The Power of Lab-Based Interview Readiness

Every successful DevOps interview shares one hidden pattern: candidates who have **real labs** behind their answers always stand out. Hiring managers can tell immediately whether a candidate has actually *done the work* or simply *read about it.*

The best preparation strategy is simple yet powerful—**Run, Record, Reflect.**

This framework trains you to:

- **Run** reproducible mini-labs that simulate real DevOps tasks.
- **Record** your process so you can explain it clearly under interview pressure.
- **Reflect** on outcomes and trade-offs to show maturity and systems thinking.

In this chapter, you'll learn how to apply this framework through **eight structured real-world labs** designed to mirror the most common DevOps interview tasks. Each lab includes a **hands-on focus**, a **narrative template** for explaining your approach in under two minutes, and insights on **how hiring panels score your performance.**

Understanding the Run, Record, Reflect Approach

Step 1: Run

Running a lab means setting up a realistic, reproducible environment. Don't just follow a tutorial—introduce small issues, break things, and fix them.

Interviewers love hearing how you handled *imperfections*, not just how you executed a perfect run.

Step 2: Record

Recording refers to documenting your thought process. Keep a personal "DevOps diary" or GitHub wiki where you log what commands you used, what went wrong, how you fixed it, and what metrics you collected. This not only deepens your memory but helps you recall details under pressure.

Step 3: Reflect

Reflection is what separates a technician from an engineer. Think about why an issue occurred, how your solution could scale, and what you'd automate next. During interviews, this reflective thinking earns high scores for maturity and ownership.

Lab 1 — Linux & Troubleshooting: Live Crash-and-Fix

Objective

Interviewers love Linux-based troubleshooting tasks because they reveal your comfort with real systems. This lab helps you simulate a small crash scenario, walk through your debugging steps, and confidently present your reasoning in an interview.

Lab Setup

Set up a lightweight Ubuntu or CentOS VM. Introduce a controlled failure such as a full disk, CPU spike, or service crash. For example, intentionally fill up disk space by creating a large dummy file and observe how system services react.

Step-by-Step Debugging Playbook

- Start by running df -h to check disk usage.

- Identify large files using du -sh * | sort -rh | head -10.
- Clear unnecessary logs in /var/log.
- Restart services and verify stability with systemctl status.

90-Second Interview Explanation Template

Step 1: Context (15 seconds)

"I simulated a production-like issue where the web service crashed due to full disk utilization. The goal was to restore service without restarting the entire instance."

Step 2: Approach (60 seconds)

"I used Linux utilities like df and du to locate large log files, archived and rotated them, and restarted only the affected services. I then verified system stability using top and systemctl status."

Step 3: Outcome (15 seconds)

"This improved uptime by avoiding full instance reboots. In interviews, I highlight that my approach was minimal-impact and diagnostic-driven rather than trial-and-error."

This concise explanation structure shows analytical calmness—a key soft skill in DevOps interviews.

Lab 2 — CI/CD Pipeline Rescue: Fix a Failing Build Under Pressure

Objective

In most DevOps interviews, you'll face a scenario where a pipeline fails minutes before deployment. Interviewers assess how you identify failure points and communicate solutions under time pressure.

Lab Setup

Use Jenkins, GitHub Actions, or GitLab CI to build a small application. Introduce an intentional syntax error or version mismatch to simulate a failing build.

Steps to Run the Lab

- Trigger the pipeline with a commit that introduces a build failure.
- Examine build logs to find the failure line.
- Reproduce the issue locally.
- Fix the configuration and push the corrected change.

How to Present During Interview

Step 1: Describe the Scenario

"I worked on a CI/CD pipeline where a build suddenly failed due to a Python dependency version mismatch."

Step 2: Explain the Thought Process

"I reviewed the pipeline logs in Jenkins, identified that the failure occurred during dependency installation, and noticed conflicting requirements between two packages. I pinned the correct versions in the requirements file and rebuilt successfully."

Step 3: Highlight the Impact

"This reduced build timeouts and improved developer confidence. I also added a pre-build validation stage to catch dependency issues early."

Bonus Tip

Mention that you implemented **pipeline logging enhancements** or **notification improvements**—these small follow-ups demonstrate ownership and proactive problem-solving, which hiring managers value highly.

Lab 3 — Infrastructure as Code: Safe Terraform Change & Rollback

Objective

Interviewers often ask about Infrastructure as Code because it tests your ability to automate without breaking production. This lab shows how to apply safe deployment and rollback using Terraform.

Lab Setup

Create a Terraform configuration for deploying a simple AWS EC2 instance or an S3 bucket. Introduce a controlled change, such as modifying instance type or adding a tag.

Step-by-Step Exercise

- Run terraform plan and review proposed changes.
- Apply the change with terraform apply.
- Simulate drift by manually altering an instance parameter in the AWS console.
- Detect drift using terraform plan again.
- Roll back the manual change safely using Terraform.

BUILD-Scored Answer Template (for Interview)

B — Background:

"I had an IaC setup in Terraform managing EC2 infrastructure."

U — Understanding the Problem:

"An engineer made a manual change outside of Terraform, causing configuration drift."

I — Implementation:

"I ran terraform plan to detect drift and restored consistency by reapplying code-defined configurations."

L — Learning:

"I highlighted the importance of avoiding manual edits and added a CI validation to run terraform validate before each merge."

D — Demonstrated Impact:

"This ensured environment consistency and reduced configuration drift incidents."

This format shows end-to-end ownership, clarity, and technical accountability.

Lab 4 — Kubernetes: Debug a Canary Deployment

Objective

Kubernetes interviews often revolve around deployment issues. Canary rollouts test how you reason about progressive delivery, service routing, and observability.

Lab Setup

Deploy two versions of a simple microservice (v1 and v2) using Kubernetes Deployment and Service manifests. Simulate a faulty version rollout that causes partial user errors.

Key Commands and Metrics

- Use kubectl get pods to verify rollout status.
- Inspect the canary deployment with kubectl describe deployment.
- Check application logs via kubectl logs.
- Monitor traffic using kubectl top pods or Prometheus metrics.

Whiteboard/Interview Narrative

Context:

"I simulated a canary rollout in Kubernetes where v2 started returning 5xx errors while v1 remained stable."

Approach:

"I used kubectl rollout status to confirm partial rollout and analyzed logs for v2 pods. Identified a missing environment variable in the deployment manifest. I rolled back using kubectl rollout undo and verified stability."

Outcome:

"This demonstrated my ability to perform safe rollouts with real-time metrics, highlighting reliability and rollback readiness."

Follow-Up Question Examples

- How do you monitor canary success criteria?
- How would you automate rollback using Helm or ArgoCD?

Answering these with practical reasoning (not theory) shows deep Kubernetes confidence.

Lab 5 — Observability & SLOs: Show Me You Can

Measure Reliability

Objective

Modern DevOps teams care deeply about observability and reliability metrics. This lab demonstrates how you define Service Level Objectives (SLOs) and defend your monitoring design.

Lab Setup

Create a simple web service (even static). Add a synthetic uptime check using Prometheus + Alertmanager or an external service like UptimeRobot.

Steps to Implement

- Define an SLO: "99.5% uptime for API responses under 500 ms."
- Set up metrics collection (e.g., response time histogram in Prometheus).
- Create an alert rule when SLO breaches exceed thresholds.
- Simulate downtime and analyze alert notifications.

Interview Presentation Script

Step 1: Context

"I built a monitoring setup for a small web API and defined an SLO around latency and uptime."

Step 2: Implementation

"I used Prometheus to track response durations and Grafana to visualize error budgets. Configured alerts to trigger when 95th percentile latency exceeded 500 ms."

Step 3: Reflection

"This exercise helped me understand trade-offs between strict alerting and false positives. In interviews, I explain how I tuned alert sensitivity to avoid noise."

Bonus: Defending Your SLO

If asked to justify your SLO, respond like this:

"The 99.5% target balances customer experience with operational capacity. Raising it to 99.9% would require significant cost in redundancy without proportional user impact."

That kind of reasoning demonstrates both technical and business understanding—a top hiring signal.

Lab 6 — Performance Triage: Small Load Test, Big Insights

Objective

Performance awareness is a critical skill. Many interviewers present performance degradation scenarios and expect you to analyze bottlenecks logically.

Lab Setup

Use tools like Apache JMeter, k6, or Locust to generate load against a simple web API.

Steps to Execute

- Design a test with 50–100 concurrent users.
- Record response time, throughput, and error rate.
- Simulate performance degradation by limiting CPU or database connections.
- Identify bottlenecks and propose solutions.

2-Minute Postmortem Presentation

Step 1: Observation (30 seconds)

"During a load test with 100 concurrent users, average response time increased from 200 ms to 900 ms."

Step 2: Diagnosis (60 seconds)

"Analyzed server metrics and found high CPU utilization and connection pool exhaustion. The database was configured with a low max_connections value."

Step 3: Solution (30 seconds)

"I tuned connection pooling, introduced caching for read-heavy endpoints, and achieved a 65% performance improvement."

This crisp presentation style communicates problem-solving agility, a major plus in senior DevOps interviews.

Lab 7 — Security & Compliance: Quick Audit and Fix Plan

Objective

Security is now integral to DevOps. Interviewers frequently test how you handle vulnerabilities and compliance checks.

Lab Setup

Run a lightweight audit on a containerized application using tools like Trivy or Docker Bench for Security. Intentionally include outdated dependencies or open ports.

Key Steps

- Scan the container image with Trivy.
- Identify high-severity vulnerabilities.

- Patch by upgrading dependencies or restricting image privileges.
- Document remediation actions.

Interview Script Example

Scenario:

"I ran a Trivy scan on our container images and found multiple high-severity vulnerabilities in base packages."

Action:

"I switched to a slim base image and upgraded dependencies to remove CVEs. Also, enforced non-root user execution in the Dockerfile."

Impact:

"This reduced the image size and eliminated high-risk vulnerabilities. In interviews, I highlight how small security hygiene steps improve compliance posture."

Follow-Up Discussion Topics

- How do you integrate security scans into CI/CD?
- What is your approach to managing secrets in pipelines?

Practical responses using examples from your own setups make your security answers credible and impressive.

Lab 8 — On-Call Simulation: Communicate, Decide, Restore

Objective

On-call simulation interviews are designed to test your decision-making, communication, and composure under pressure. This lab prepares you for that moment.

Lab Setup

Simulate a production outage in your local environment—perhaps by taking down a service or blocking network access temporarily. Set a timeline for restoring service while communicating status updates.

Steps to Practice

- Document the incident timeline.
- Use clear, timestamped communication logs: "12:01 – Incident detected; 12:03 – Initial diagnosis; 12:10 – Root cause identified."
- Restore service and document lessons learned.

Communication Template

Step 1: Situation Summary

"At 12:01, API latency increased sharply. I alerted the team and began checking recent deployments."

Step 2: Diagnosis and Action

"Identified a misconfigured environment variable in a new deployment. Rolled back using the previous container image."

Step 3: Communication and Learning

"Kept stakeholders informed every 10 minutes. After resolution, added pre-deployment checks for environment configuration validation."

Scoring Example

Hiring teams use communication clarity as a leadership indicator. They often score responses based on:

- Calmness and tone during explanation
- Structured updates under time pressure
- Balance between action and communication

If you demonstrate composure through a clear narrative, you automatically signal readiness for real operational responsibility.

Bringing It All Together: The Reflective Layer

Running labs and explaining them effectively are just the first two steps. Reflection is what turns a technician into a thought leader. After completing all eight labs, document your key reflections.

Ask yourself:

- What did I learn about diagnosing under pressure?
- Which tools increased my speed or accuracy?
- How can I automate this process for the next time?

Keep a concise reflection log in your Git repository. When interviewers ask, "What's your biggest DevOps learning so far?", your reflection becomes your answer.

Final Thoughts: Labs as Interview Superpowers

These eight labs are not just technical exercises—they are **confidence-building simulations** that mirror the daily challenges of DevOps professionals.

By mastering the **Run, Record, Reflect** framework, you transform your preparation from passive reading into active storytelling. You will be able to:

- Speak with authority because you've lived the scenarios.
- Demonstrate reliability under simulated stress.
- Articulate trade-offs like a seasoned engineer.

When interviewers ask, "Can you walk us through something you've built or debugged recently?", you'll have eight powerful, ready-to-present case studies that show your practical strength and reflective maturity.

In DevOps interviews, the strongest candidates are not the ones who know the most tools—they are the ones who can **explain real impact clearly**.

Your labs are the bridge between knowing and showing.

Lab 1 — Linux & Troubleshooting: Live Crash and Fix

Why Linux Troubleshooting Dominates DevOps Interviews

Every DevOps professional eventually faces a live system crash. Services fail, resources get exhausted, and business applications slow down at the worst possible moment. This is why Linux troubleshooting remains the backbone of almost every DevOps technical interview.

When interviewers bring up Linux problems, they are not testing how many commands you can remember. They are assessing how you think when things go wrong, how you communicate under pressure, and whether you can restore stability without panic.

This chapter prepares you to perform and explain troubleshooting tasks in a way that makes hiring managers immediately trust your operational confidence.

The Interviewer's Real Evaluation Criteria

When a hiring panel gives you a troubleshooting problem, they are silently evaluating three dimensions of your skillset.

Structured Thinking

They want to see whether you approach the issue in a calm, systematic manner. The best candidates always start by understanding the problem, confirming the scope, and identifying where the failure begins before they take any corrective action.

Tool Fluency

They observe if you are comfortable using Linux tools such as top, journalctl, df, or ss to gather real data rather than guessing. The way you reach for the right tool shows your level of practical exposure.

Composure Under Pressure

A large part of troubleshooting is staying calm. If you can communicate clearly while resolving a problem, it tells the interviewer that you will remain stable during production incidents in real life.

If you display these three traits, you can score highly even if your technical answer is not perfect. Interviewers value your method more than memorization.

Typical Interview Scenario

One of the most common Linux questions sounds simple but tests your complete debugging mindset.

Imagine an interviewer says:

"Your web application suddenly stops responding. Users report 500 errors. You have SSH access to the Linux host. Walk me through what you do next."

Your answer must balance **logic, confidence, and speed.** The next sections will help you build that response, backed by an actual lab simulation you can practice before any DevOps interview.

Setting Up the Troubleshooting Lab

The Practice Environment

You do not need a production setup to practice. A single Linux VM is enough. Ubuntu, Debian, or CentOS work well. You can run it locally on VirtualBox or remotely on a cloud instance.

Essential Utilities

Install and learn these standard Linux diagnostic tools. They are part of nearly every DevOps interview discussion.

htop or top – Monitor CPU, memory, and process behavior.

journalctl and systemctl – Investigate systemd service status and logs.

df and du – Identify disk usage and storage distribution.

ss or netstat – Observe network connections and port bindings.

dmesg – View kernel-level or hardware error messages.

Knowing when and why to use each of these tools is far more important than listing all their options.

Simulating a Crash

Real learning happens when you break things intentionally. The goal is to reproduce common crash conditions and then recover them methodically.

Disk Full Condition

This is one of the simplest but most realistic issues that can take down a system.

Create a dummy file to fill the disk.

fallocate -l 5G /tmp/fillfile

Verify space usage.

df -h

Try restarting a service such as Apache or Nginx. It will fail with an error similar to "No space left on device."

Identify which directory or file is consuming space.

du -sh /* | sort -rh | head -10

Clean up unnecessary files or rotate logs.

Restart services and confirm stability.

Practicing this once or twice helps you explain disk troubleshooting logically in interviews.

High CPU Utilization

Another common issue is a system that becomes sluggish due to a CPU spike.

Install the stress package.

sudo apt install stress

Simulate load.

stress—cpu 4—timeout 60

Open a separate terminal and run top or htop to observe the spike.

Terminate processes and describe the recovery path.

Network Latency

Use tc (Traffic Control) to create artificial delay.

Introduce delay.

sudo tc qdisc add dev eth0 root netem delay 200ms

Run ping or curl commands to notice latency.

Remove delay.

sudo tc qdisc del dev eth0 root netem

After performing such simulations, you will have tangible examples to discuss during troubleshooting interviews.

The Ninety Second Answer Framework

When an interviewer asks how you handled a live issue, you have about ninety seconds to tell your story. Use a clear structure so your answer sounds confident and complete.

Step One: Context

Start by explaining what failed and what the visible symptom was.

Example: "A critical web service stopped responding due to high CPU utilization."

Step Two: Investigation

Explain the exact process you used to identify the cause.

"I connected via SSH, ran top to check running processes, and noticed a Java process consuming 100 percent CPU. I verified logs with journalctl and found thread creation errors."

Step Three: Solution and Validation

Describe how you restored service.

"I gracefully stopped the process, cleared temporary cache files, and restarted the service. Then I monitored CPU usage to confirm stability."

Step Four: Reflection

Add what you learned or automated afterward.

"I implemented CPU usage alerts in Prometheus and added restart protection in systemd so that similar spikes would self-recover."

This sequence keeps your answer natural yet organized and helps hiring teams score you highly on communication and clarity.

The Core Troubleshooting Methodology

Every Linux troubleshooting workflow follows a logical flow that mirrors how real engineers operate in production.

Step One: Identify the Symptom

Confirm what exactly is not working before doing anything else. Gather visible data. Use service status, log entries, and network checks.

Example commands:

systemctl status nginx

journalctl -u nginx—since "10 minutes ago"

ping localhost

curl http://127.0.0.1

Step Two: Isolate the Root Cause

Once you have evidence, narrow down the issue.

Ask yourself whether it is caused by hardware, system configuration, or external dependency failure.

Check resource utilization with top or free -m.

Check disk status with df -h.

Check open ports with ss -tuln.

Step Three: Implement Minimum Impact Fix

Avoid rebooting immediately. Apply focused fixes that minimize user impact.

Restart only the affected service or unload unnecessary processes.

Step Four: Validate and Prevent Recurrence

Always verify that your fix worked. Confirm metrics returned to normal. Then explain to your interviewer what preventive measure you implemented, such as alerting or log rotation.

Common Troubleshooting Patterns

Service Fails to Start

If asked, "Your service is not starting, what will you check first?" you can respond as follows.

Check service status using systemctl status.

Read error logs using journalctl.

Inspect port conflicts using ss -tuln | grep 80.

Fix configuration issues and restart.

Explain these steps calmly and mention that you verify the root cause rather than relying on blind restarts.

High Load Average

When a system's load average remains abnormally high, your answer should show analytical reasoning.

Confirm load with uptime or top.

Differentiate between CPU or I/O load using iostat or vmstat.

Identify processes with ps aux—sort=-%cpu.

Optimize or terminate runaway tasks.

Application Slowness

A well-rounded answer goes beyond Linux metrics and connects system and application layers.

Validate system health using top and free -m.

Check network latency with ping or traceroute.

Review application logs for timeouts.

Correlate findings with performance monitoring dashboards if available.

This blend of system and service awareness is what interviewers expect from a DevOps engineer.

How to Demonstrate Troubleshooting During Interviews

Verbal Walkthroughs

Most DevOps interviews are conversational. You might not have a terminal but will need to describe what you would do.

Use conditional phrasing to show logical thought flow.

Example:

"If the service was down, I would start by checking systemctl status. If logs show resource errors, I would use top to confirm memory or CPU bottlenecks."

This phrasing demonstrates diagnostic reasoning rather than guesswork.

Whiteboard Scenario

If you are given a diagram or asked to walk through an outage, explain how you'd trace the problem across layers.

You might say, "First, I'd confirm whether the host itself is reachable. Then I'd check if dependent services such as databases or APIs are functioning. Once the root layer is confirmed healthy, I'd move up to application logs."

Your structure shows that you can isolate layers quickly under stress.

Communication Style During Crisis

Interviewers pay close attention to your communication style when discussing incidents. Calm and clear communication is often scored separately from technical ability.

Speak in complete but short sentences. State what you observed, what you did, and what you confirmed.

Example:

"I noticed system memory usage at 98 percent. I verified that swap was also full. I restarted the log rotation service to clear residual files. Memory dropped back to 40 percent."

This type of narrative reflects professionalism and leadership potential.

Avoid emotional language such as "everything broke." Instead, use factual statements like "service became unresponsive after log files filled the partition."

Reflection and Prevention Mindset

After every crash simulation, spend time thinking about how you would prevent the same issue from returning. This reflection layer differentiates experienced engineers from new ones.

The prevention mindset involves three steps:

Monitor. Implement system metrics for CPU, disk, and service uptime.

Automate. Add cleanup scripts or service recovery triggers.

Document. Maintain incident records for future learning.

Interviewers appreciate candidates who not only fix problems but also design safeguards.

Case Study Example

Consider the following realistic incident scenario.

A web API hosted on a Linux server suddenly stops responding. Users begin reporting failures.

Step One: Observation

The first SSH login feels slow. Running top reveals a Java process consuming 100 percent CPU.

Step Two: Analysis

journalctl logs show repeated thread creation errors from the application.

Step Three: Fix

Gracefully stop the process, restart the service, and monitor CPU.

Step Four: Validation and Learning

Identify root cause: thread pool configuration error. Collaborate with developers to adjust limits and deploy a patch.

Step Five: Prevention

Add monitoring alerts for CPU and memory.

If you narrate this case in an interview using the same structure, you communicate technical skill, operational calmness, and cross-team collaboration ability.

Practicing the 90 Second Explanation

Use this exercise to prepare for real interviews.

Prompt: "Your server shows 95 percent disk usage, and some services have stopped. How will you fix it?"

Your spoken answer should include:

1. The symptom you observed.
2. The commands you used to diagnose.
3. The recovery steps you took.
4. How you verified and prevented future issues.

Record your response and time it. The goal is to sound calm, confident, and clear within ninety seconds.

How Hiring Teams Score Troubleshooting Rounds

Companies often use an internal scorecard to evaluate DevOps troubleshooting candidates.

Technical accuracy contributes around forty percent.

Clarity of explanation contributes about twenty five percent.

Calmness under pressure contributes twenty percent.

Preventive thinking contributes fifteen percent.

You can still perform strongly even if you miss a minor technical step, as long as your reasoning and communication are consistent.

Advanced Troubleshooting Topics for Senior Interviews

When interviewing for senior DevOps or SRE roles, expect questions that go beyond service restarts.

Kernel Panic Recovery – Use dmesg and analyze logs under /var/crash.

File System Corruption – Understand fsck repair operations and safe recovery methods.

Security Denials – Diagnose SELinux or AppArmor rejections via audit logs.

Process Deadlocks – Use strace to trace system calls and identify stuck threads.

Mentioning that you have practiced these advanced scenarios in your personal lab makes your profile immediately stronger.

Lessons Learned from the Linux Troubleshooting Lab

You now have a full cycle understanding of how to perform and explain troubleshooting.

Observe before acting. Always gather facts first.

Explain cause and effect clearly when answering.

Demonstrate the business or user impact of your fix.

End your answer with how you automated or prevented recurrence.

These principles apply across all DevOps interview questions.

From Command Executor to Systems Thinker

Troubleshooting is not about remembering commands; it is about diagnosing systems.

When you can describe how you analyzed an issue, restored functionality, and prevented future downtime, you demonstrate end-to-end ownership—the mindset every DevOps team values.

Through this Linux Live Crash and Fix lab, you now have a repeatable structure to practice real-time debugging and confidently communicate your approach during any DevOps interview.

By combining clear observation, systematic action, and thoughtful reflection, you become more than just a problem fixer—you become a systems thinker ready for production-scale challenges.

Lab 2 — CI/CD Pipeline Rescue: Fix a Failing Build Under Pressure

Why Pipeline Failures Define Your DevOps Maturity

Continuous Integration and Continuous Delivery (CI/CD) pipelines are the heartbeat of modern software delivery. Every code commit passes through them before reaching production. When pipelines fail, developers halt, releases freeze, and business delivery suffers. In DevOps interviews, troubleshooting a failing CI/CD build is one of the most realistic and high-impact exercises used to assess a candidate's hands-on capability.

Interviewers use CI/CD troubleshooting scenarios to measure whether you truly understand the automation backbone that powers software delivery. They want to see how you handle uncertainty, how you prioritize steps under pressure, and how you communicate recovery actions in real time.

If you can confidently walk an interviewer through how you detect, diagnose, and fix a broken pipeline, you instantly differentiate yourself from candidates who only know the tools superficially.

What Interviewers Look For in CI/CD Troubleshooting Rounds

During a CI/CD failure simulation or discussion, hiring managers silently score you across four key traits.

Observational Clarity

Do you start by verifying where the failure occurs — build, test, or deploy stage — before diving into solutions?

Technical Fluency

Can you read pipeline logs, interpret error messages, and relate them to underlying configuration or environment issues?

Calm Decision Making

Can you explain your next step clearly when something unexpected happens under time pressure?

Recovery and Prevention Thinking

Do you not only fix the issue but also discuss how to prevent recurrence through pipeline hardening, caching strategies, or better environment isolation?

The ideal candidate communicates both control and curiosity. They do not rush into fixes but narrate their reasoning with confidence.

The Typical Interview Scenario

A classic DevOps interview exercise begins like this:

"The CI/CD pipeline for your application suddenly starts failing. Developers are blocked from merging code because builds keep breaking. You have access to the logs and YAML configuration. Walk us through how you would investigate and fix the issue."

Your ability to structure that answer — not your ability to remember every Jenkins or GitHub Actions setting — determines your evaluation. The interviewer wants to see your mental model of debugging under production-like stress.

Let's explore how to build that model through a hands-on, real-world lab that you can practice independently before any interview.

The CI/CD Pipeline Rescue Lab

Objective

In this lab, you will simulate a failing CI/CD pipeline, identify the cause using logs, and fix the configuration while explaining your reasoning in a way that impresses hiring managers.

You will learn how to:

- Recognize failure patterns in build logs.
- Apply systematic debugging to pipeline scripts.
- Communicate your recovery strategy using a concise, interview-ready format.

Setting Up a Sample Pipeline

You can use either Jenkins or GitHub Actions for this exercise. Both offer a strong foundation for understanding modern CI/CD behavior.

Example Setup Using GitHub Actions

Create a simple pipeline YAML file named .github/workflows/build.yml.

```
name: Build and Test

on:

push:

branches: [ "main" ]

jobs:

build:

runs-on: ubuntu-latest
```

```
steps:

- name: Checkout code

uses: actions/checkout@v3

- name: Install dependencies

run: npm install

- name: Run tests

run: npm test
```

This simple workflow runs automatically on every push to the main branch. Now imagine that the npm test step fails due to an environment issue. In a live interview, this is exactly the kind of scenario you'll be asked to walk through.

Simulating a Failure

To make the lab realistic, deliberately introduce an error in the pipeline. For instance, change the dependency command to an invalid one:

```
run: npm installl
```

When the pipeline executes, it fails with a message such as:

```
npm: command not found

Error: Process completed with exit code 127
```

At this point, the interviewer might say: "Your pipeline build has failed with this error. What will you do next?"

This is your cue to begin the structured rescue explanation.

The 90-Second Rescue Framework

When answering any CI/CD troubleshooting question in an interview, use a structured 90-second narrative that covers four stages.

Step One: Describe the Symptom

"I observed that the CI pipeline failed during the dependency installation stage with an error stating 'npm command not found.' The failure occurred before tests began, indicating a setup or environment issue."

Step Two: Diagnose the Root Cause

"I checked the build logs to confirm which step failed. The error appeared right after the runner initialization, so I examined the YAML configuration and noticed a typo in the install command. I also verified that Node.js was not being installed before npm was used."

Step Three: Apply the Fix

"I added a step to install Node.js before running npm commands and corrected the spelling of the install command. Then I re-triggered the workflow to validate the fix."

- name: Setup Node.js

uses: actions/setup-node@v3

with:

node-version: 18

- name: Install dependencies

run: npm install

Step Four: Reflect and Prevent

"I updated the pipeline to include linting of YAML files as part of pre-commit checks and documented environment requirements in the repository README. This prevents similar errors during future builds."

This concise framework demonstrates situational awareness, technical accuracy, and ownership — exactly what hiring panels want.

Understanding Real Build Failure Categories

Every CI/CD system, whether Jenkins, GitLab CI, or GitHub Actions, tends to fail within a few predictable categories. Understanding these categories gives you a foundation for structured diagnosis.

Configuration Errors

Incorrect YAML or Jenkinsfile syntax, missing environment variables, or referencing steps in the wrong order often cause builds to fail before execution even begins.

Example symptoms include parsing errors like mapping values are not allowed or "stage not found." These indicate configuration structure issues.

Dependency or Environment Errors

When the pipeline cannot install required packages or cannot find a tool in the build agent, it fails during the preparation phase. This often happens when the runner image is missing dependencies or when caching is misconfigured.

Test Failures

Tests might fail due to application bugs or environment inconsistencies. Distinguishing between code defects and infrastructure issues shows analytical maturity.

Permission and Secret Failures

Missing tokens, expired credentials, or restricted permissions can cause deployment stages to fail. Understanding secret management best practices makes your answers stand out.

External Service Failures

Sometimes the failure originates outside your pipeline — such as an unavailable Docker registry or cloud API throttling. In interviews, explaining that you check both internal and external factors demonstrates systems thinking.

Example: Jenkins Build Fails After SCM Checkout

Consider this real-world scenario. A Jenkins job fails immediately after source checkout with the following log message:

ERROR: Error cloning remote repo 'origin'

hudson.plugins.git.GitException: Command "git fetch—tags—progress" returned status code 128

An interviewer might ask, "How do you troubleshoot this?"

The logical answer path would sound like this:

1. Acknowledge that the issue occurs during source control checkout, before build execution.
2. Verify repository URL configuration in Jenkins and test manual git access using the same credentials.
3. Check whether the build agent has proper SSH keys or HTTPS credentials.
4. Identify if the branch name has changed or the token has expired.
5. Once fixed, re-trigger the build and confirm the checkout succeeds.

In your spoken explanation, you must show the interviewer that you can quickly isolate which layer — SCM, Jenkins configuration, or credential store — is responsible.

Communicating During a CI/CD Outage

When discussing incident scenarios, interviewers value not just what you fix but how you communicate under pressure. During a real pipeline failure, developers, managers, and release engineers all depend on clear updates.

Explain that your first step is to acknowledge the impact: "All builds for main are currently failing."

Next, describe the isolation step: "The failure is limited to the build stage, not deployments."

Then describe the immediate workaround: "Developers can continue working on feature branches while we restore main pipeline functionality."

This demonstrates both technical skill and team coordination capability, which are core DevOps qualities.

Practice Exercise: Diagnosing a Failing Build Log

Here is a realistic build log snippet. Read it as if you are in a live interview.

Step 3/4 : RUN pip install -r requirements.txt

ERROR: Could not find a version that satisfies the requirement requests==2.32.0 (from versions: none)

ERROR: No matching distribution found for requests==2.32.0

An interviewer might ask, "What do you think went wrong here?"

Your thought process should sound like this:

"The error indicates a dependency resolution problem. The requirements file may reference a package version that doesn't exist in PyPI. I would first verify the requirements file, confirm internet access from the build agent, and check if there's a typo in the version number."

Then you could add: "After correcting the version, I would rebuild the container and re-run the job to confirm success."

This kind of answer shows you can interpret logs logically and propose a fix without panic.

Understanding Pipeline Caching and Artifacts

Interviewers often dig deeper by asking how you would optimize or stabilize CI/CD performance after a fix. This leads to discussions on caching and artifact management.

Explain that caching prevents redundant package downloads, reducing both time and risk of network-related failures. In GitHub Actions, you can add caching like this:

```
- name: Cache node modules

uses: actions/cache@v3

with:

path: ~/.npm

key: ${{ runner.os }}-node-${{ hashFiles('package-lock.json') }}

restore-keys: |

${{ runner.os }}-node-
```

You can highlight that after enabling caching, the build becomes faster and less dependent on external network conditions. This demonstrates practical optimization insight beyond simple debugging.

Common Mistakes Candidates Make During Pipeline Questions

Guessing Without Reading Logs

Some candidates start suggesting random fixes instead of examining log output. Interviewers notice this immediately. Always start with observation.

Ignoring Environment Context

A fix that works locally may not work in the build environment. Always mention that you check the container image or build agent setup.

Overlooking Rollback and Verification

After fixing a pipeline, you should explain how you verify stability — for example, rerunning the pipeline or comparing build durations before and after.

Advanced Scenario: Deployment Step Fails in Production

Imagine this sequence: the build completes successfully, tests pass, but the deployment stage fails with the following log.

Error: Permission denied while trying to access the S3 bucket.

AccessDenied: Access Denied

A strong response would go like this:

"I first verify whether the AWS credentials injected into the pipeline are valid. I check the IAM role attached to the runner or Jenkins agent to ensure it has the correct S3 permissions. If credentials have rotated, I update the secret store. Then I rerun only the deploy stage to confirm the fix."

Adding that you would implement automated credential rotation monitoring shows awareness of secure DevOps practices.

The Reflective Layer: Turning Failure into Learning

In interviews, after you describe the technical resolution, interviewers often ask, "What did you learn from that incident?" This is where your reflection adds maturity.

You could say: "I learned that validating environment dependencies early in the pipeline prevents cascading failures. Since then, I've added pre-flight checks and parallelized dependency installations to improve reliability."

Reflection demonstrates not only skill but growth mindset — a top trait companies seek in DevOps professionals.

Presenting CI/CD Fixes During System Design or Whiteboard Rounds

Sometimes, CI/CD questions appear during broader design discussions. For example, you might be asked how you would design a reliable deployment system.

Here, combine practical and architectural insight. Start with:

"I'd design the pipeline in stages — build, test, security scan, and deploy. Each stage would have clear success criteria. Failures in earlier stages prevent promotion."

Then, mention you'd integrate notification hooks and rollback steps:

"I would configure the pipeline to send Slack or Teams alerts upon failure and implement automated rollbacks in case deployments exceed error thresholds."

Your goal is to show that you think about reliability from both operational and automation perspectives.

Real Interview Question Examples

"Your pipeline suddenly takes twice as long as usual. How do you approach the investigation?"

Explain that you'd compare build durations over the last few runs, check caching effectiveness, and identify if any step recently changed (for example, dependency installation updates).

"The Jenkins agent reports disk full errors during build. What will you do?"

Respond by describing how you'd clean up old workspace directories, prune Docker images, and set up periodic cleanup jobs.

"GitHub Actions workflow works for you but fails for teammates. Why?"

Explain that the issue may be due to missing repository secrets, branch protection rules, or workflow triggers that depend on specific access permissions.

The Interview Demonstration Strategy

When given a laptop or shared environment during an interview, your focus should not be on finishing tasks fastest but on demonstrating visibility. Talk as you type. Narrate your reasoning.

For example, say: "I'm first checking which stage failed by opening the Actions log. It looks like the test stage never started, meaning the build failed earlier. I'll verify if dependencies were installed."

This continuous verbalization gives interviewers insight into your structured reasoning and confidence.

Building Preventive Maturity

The highest-scoring candidates do not stop at fixes. They discuss preventive measures such as:

- Validating YAML syntax with pre-commit hooks.
- Enabling pipeline linting tools.
- Configuring test runners to produce structured reports.
- Monitoring build durations and failure rates with metrics dashboards.

Explaining that you implement such controls indicates readiness for production-scale environments.

Lessons Learned from the CI/CD Rescue Lab

The true lesson of pipeline troubleshooting is not memorization of commands but development of diagnostic intuition. You should now be able to explain the lifecycle of a pipeline failure — from symptom to recovery — with clarity.

You learned how to interpret logs rather than panic, how to repair YAML configuration issues calmly, and how to communicate your progress during an outage. You also learned how to describe post-mortem actions and preventive improvements.

The more you practice this pattern, the faster and more confident your responses become during interviews.

Closing Reflection: Pressure as a DevOps Skill

Pipeline failures simulate production pressure. Interviewers deliberately create these conditions to observe how you handle complexity when automation breaks. They want to know if you are a firefighter or an engineer who can remain methodical amid the flames.

By mastering CI/CD rescue scenarios, you transform panic into process, chaos into clarity, and stress into structure. When you can calmly walk through a broken build, explain what went wrong, demonstrate how you fixed it, and outline how you'd prevent it from happening again, you embody the essence of DevOps professionalism.

This lab gives you both the vocabulary and confidence to excel in those moments. Every command you type and every explanation you give becomes a signal that you're not just familiar with CI/CD — you're prepared to lead it under pressure.

Lab 3 — Infrastructure as Code: Safe Terraform Change & Rollback

Introduction to Infrastructure as Code

Infrastructure as Code (IaC) has transformed the way modern IT operations and DevOps teams manage infrastructure. Traditional infrastructure management was largely manual, error-prone, and slow. IaC allows teams to define infrastructure using declarative configuration files, making deployments predictable, repeatable, and version-controlled.

Terraform, developed by HashiCorp, is one of the most popular IaC tools. It enables DevOps engineers to provision and manage cloud resources safely and efficiently. One of the key challenges in using Terraform in production environments is implementing changes safely and rolling back in case of errors. This chapter will focus on strategies, best practices, and real-time interview-oriented examples to manage Terraform changes safely and perform rollbacks effectively.

Understanding Terraform State and Its Importance

Terraform maintains a state file, which is crucial for tracking infrastructure resources. The state file maps the resources defined in your Terraform configuration to the real-world infrastructure. This mapping ensures that Terraform knows what has been created, updated, or destroyed.

A deep understanding of Terraform state is essential for safe infrastructure changes because:

- It allows Terraform to plan changes accurately.
- It prevents accidental deletion of critical resources.

- It enables safe collaboration among multiple engineers by using remote state storage.

Remote State Management

In real-world scenarios, managing Terraform state locally can be risky. Remote state management solves this problem by storing the state in a shared, secure backend. AWS S3, Terraform Cloud, and HashiCorp Consul are popular choices for remote state storage.

For example, configuring a remote state backend in AWS S3 looks like this:

```
terraform {

backend "s3" {

bucket = "devops-terraform-state"

key = "lab3/terraform.tfstate"

region = "us-east-1"

}

}
```

Using remote state ensures that team members always have access to the latest state file, reducing the risk of conflicts during infrastructure changes.

Planning Safe Terraform Changes

The core principle of safe Terraform changes is to preview the effects before applying them. Terraform provides the terraform plan command to generate an execution plan.

- terraform plan will compare the current state file with the desired configuration and show the differences.

- This step is essential for interviews because real-world scenarios often test your ability to detect potential destructive changes.

Example scenario:

You have a live AWS EC2 instance running a critical web application. The team wants to increase the instance size from t2.micro to t2.medium. Running terraform plan will display:

- The current instance type.
- The proposed instance type.
- Whether Terraform will destroy and recreate the resource or perform an in-place update.

Using Terraform Plan Effectively

- Always use terraform plan -out=tfplan to save the plan to a file.
- Review the plan thoroughly, especially for changes marked as - (destroy) and + (create).
- For large teams, sharing the plan file ensures that all members understand the upcoming changes.

Example:

terraform plan -out=tfplan

terraform show tfplan

This sequence allows you to inspect the plan before execution, giving you confidence that changes are safe.

Applying Terraform Changes Safely

Once the plan is reviewed, you can apply the changes using terraform apply. However, blindly applying changes without safeguards is a common mistake in real-world operations.

Strategies for Safe Application

- Use workspaces for environment segregation. Terraform workspaces allow you to maintain multiple environments such as development, staging, and production from the same configuration.

- Implement approval gates. In production, it's recommended to require manual approval before applying changes.

- Limit destructive actions. You can use the -target flag to apply changes to specific resources rather than the entire configuration.

Example:

terraform apply -target=aws_instance.web_server

This ensures that only the web server instance is updated while leaving other resources untouched.

Handling Terraform Rollbacks

Rollback in Terraform is not as straightforward as traditional database rollback because infrastructure changes can be destructive. However, there are multiple strategies to mitigate risks and restore the previous state.

Using Version Control for Configurations

Store all Terraform configurations in Git. Before applying any changes:

- Create a new branch for your changes.

- Commit the current working configuration.

- Use pull requests to review changes.

If something goes wrong after applying changes, you can revert the branch and reapply the previous configuration.

Using Terraform State Snapshots

Terraform allows you to backup the state file before applying changes. This is especially useful in production environments. For example:

cp terraform.tfstate terraform.tfstate.backup

If a deployment fails or causes unintended changes, you can restore the previous state:

mv terraform.tfstate.backup terraform.tfstate

terraform apply

Blue-Green and Canary Deployments

For critical infrastructure like load balancers or database clusters, blue-green or canary deployment strategies can serve as effective rollback mechanisms.

- Blue-Green Deployment: Maintain two identical environments. Deploy new changes to the inactive environment. If successful, switch traffic. If not, rollback is instantaneous.

- Canary Deployment: Deploy changes to a small portion of your infrastructure first. Monitor the outcome before scaling changes to the entire environment.

Common Interview Questions and Practical Scenarios

Interviewers often test your practical understanding of safe Terraform changes and rollbacks with scenario-based questions. Here are a few examples:

Scenario 1: Accidental Deletion of Resources

Question: You applied a Terraform plan that inadvertently marked a production database for destruction. How do you handle this?

Answer:

- Immediately stop further Terraform operations.
- Restore the previous state from backup.
- Use terraform import to reattach any manually recreated resources.
- Apply changes carefully with targeted resources.

Scenario 2: Conflicting Changes by Team Members

Question: Two engineers modified the same Terraform resource in different branches. How do you avoid state conflicts?

Answer:

- Use remote state with locking enabled.
- Review the plan thoroughly before applying.
- Merge changes in Git with proper pull requests and conflict resolution.

Scenario 3: Infrastructure Drift Detection

Question: How do you detect if your live infrastructure has drifted from the Terraform configuration?

Answer:

- Run terraform plan without applying changes. Terraform will show any drift as +/- operations.

- Periodically schedule drift detection in automated pipelines.

Real-Time Practical Example

Let's walk through a complete practical example demonstrating safe Terraform changes and rollback.

Scenario: You want to add a new AWS S3 bucket and increase the size of an existing EC2 instance.

1. Initialize Terraform:

terraform init

1. Create a plan and save it:

terraform plan -out=tfplan

1. Review the plan:

terraform show tfplan

1. Apply changes:

terraform apply tfplan

1. Detect issues post-apply:

terraform plan

1. If issues are detected, rollback:

mv terraform.tfstate.backup terraform.tfstate

terraform apply

This example highlights a real-time, step-by-step approach that interviewers expect candidates to understand.

Best Practices for Terraform Changes and Rollbacks

Use Modular Configurations

Modularize Terraform code to isolate components. This allows you to apply changes to specific modules without affecting unrelated resources.

Implement Continuous Integration

Integrate Terraform with CI/CD pipelines. This allows automated plan generation, approval, and safe application in non-production environments.

Automate Backups

Schedule automatic backups of state files to prevent data loss and enable quick rollbacks.

Document Every Change

Maintain a change log for Terraform deployments. This demonstrates professionalism and is often discussed in interviews as a key aspect of safe operations.

Safe Terraform change management and rollback are critical skills for any DevOps engineer. By mastering state management, plan inspection, targeted application, rollback strategies, and modular coding, you can ensure infrastructure reliability and reduce operational risks. Real-time scenarios, such as accidental resource deletion or drift detection, are frequently discussed in interviews, so having practical examples ready is essential.

Lab 4 — Kubernetes: Debug a Canary Deployment

Introduction to Canary Deployments

Canary deployments are a critical strategy in modern DevOps practices for releasing updates to applications in a controlled manner. The term "canary" comes from the practice of sending a canary bird into coal mines to detect harmful gases. In software deployment, a small subset of users receives the new version first, allowing teams to monitor behavior, identify potential issues, and roll back if necessary, without impacting the majority of users.

Kubernetes, the leading container orchestration platform, provides a robust environment to implement canary deployments using Deployments, ReplicaSets, Services, and advanced routing mechanisms. Understanding how to deploy, monitor, and debug canary releases is a highly practical skill frequently tested in DevOps interviews.

This chapter is focused on practical real-time strategies for debugging a Kubernetes canary deployment and ensuring smooth, safe updates.

Kubernetes Deployment Concepts for Canary Releases

Before diving into debugging, it is essential to understand key Kubernetes concepts related to canary deployments:

Deployments

Deployments are declarative configurations used to manage stateless applications in Kubernetes. They define the desired state of pods and handle scaling, rolling updates, and rollbacks automatically.

ReplicaSets

ReplicaSets ensure that a specified number of pod replicas are running at any given time. While Deployments manage ReplicaSets, understanding their behavior is crucial for debugging canaries.

Services

Services expose pods to internal or external clients. In canary deployments, services must support selective routing to direct a fraction of traffic to the new version.

Labels and Selectors

Labels are key-value pairs attached to pods, and selectors determine which pods are targeted by a service or Deployment. Labeling is the backbone of canary deployments because it allows routing traffic to specific versions of an application.

Setting Up a Canary Deployment in Kubernetes

Let's walk through a practical example of setting up a canary deployment.

Step 1: Deploy the Stable Version

Create a Deployment for the stable version of your application:

```
apiVersion: apps/v1

kind: Deployment

metadata:

name: webapp-stable

spec:

replicas: 3

selector:
```

```yaml
matchLabels:
app: webapp
version: stable
template:
metadata:
labels:
app: webapp
version: stable
spec:
containers:
- name: webapp
image: myregistry/webapp:1.0.0
ports:
- containerPort: 80
```

Apply the configuration:

```
kubectl apply -f webapp-stable.yaml
```

Verify pods are running:

```
kubectl get pods -l app=webapp
```

Step 2: Deploy the Canary Version

Deploy a new version alongside the stable version:

```yaml
apiVersion: apps/v1
```

```yaml
kind: Deployment
metadata:
name: webapp-canary
spec:
replicas: 1
selector:
matchLabels:
app: webapp
version: canary
template:
metadata:
labels:
app: webapp
version: canary
spec:
containers:
- name: webapp
image: myregistry/webapp:1.1.0
ports:
- containerPort: 80
```

Apply the canary deployment:

```
kubectl apply -f webapp-canary.yaml
```

Step 3: Configure the Service

Update the service to route traffic to both stable and canary pods. Kubernetes' default round-robin Service can be used, or more advanced traffic splitting tools like Istio or Linkerd can provide weighted routing.

For default routing:

```
apiVersion: v1

kind: Service

metadata:

name: webapp-service

spec:

selector:

app: webapp

ports:

- protocol: TCP

port: 80

targetPort: 80

type: ClusterIP
```

Apply the service:

```
kubectl apply -f webapp-service.yaml
```

At this stage, 3 stable pods and 1 canary pod are receiving traffic.

Common Issues in Canary Deployments

Debugging canary deployments requires a clear understanding of potential problems. Interviewers often test your ability to identify and solve these issues in real-time scenarios.

Issue 1: Pods Not Running

Symptom: The canary pod fails to start or crashes immediately.

Solution:

- Inspect pod logs:

```
kubectl logs <pod-name>
```

- Check events for scheduling or image pull errors:

```
kubectl describe pod <pod-name>
```

- Verify the container image exists and the image tag is correct.
- Confirm resource requests and limits are reasonable.

Issue 2: Traffic Not Reaching Canary Pods

Symptom: Users are not routed to the new version even though the pod is running.

Solution:

- Verify labels and selectors:

```
kubectl get pods—show-labels
kubectl describe service webapp-service
```

- Ensure the service selector includes both stable and canary labels.

- For advanced routing, validate Istio VirtualService or Linkerd routing rules.

Issue 3: Resource Constraints

Symptom: Canary pods are evicted or fail to start due to insufficient CPU or memory.

Solution:

- Check pod events:

```
kubectl describe pod <canary-pod-name>
```

- Adjust resource requests and limits in the Deployment configuration.
- Ensure nodes have enough available resources.

Issue 4: Application Errors in Canary Version

Symptom: Application is serving errors to users.

Solution:

- Analyze pod logs:

```
kubectl logs <canary-pod-name>
```

- Use Kubernetes exec to debug inside the pod:

```
kubectl exec -it <canary-pod-name>—/bin/bash
```

- Compare configurations between stable and canary versions to identify differences causing the failure.

Monitoring Canary Deployments

Effective monitoring is critical for canary deployments. Interviewers expect candidates to know how to detect issues before they impact users.

Metrics to Monitor

- Pod health and readiness
- CPU and memory usage
- Request success and failure rates
- Latency and response times
- Error logs

Tools for Monitoring

- Prometheus and Grafana for metrics visualization
- Kubernetes Dashboard for real-time pod status
- Istio or Linkerd telemetry for advanced traffic analysis

Example: Checking pod metrics with Prometheus query

```
sum(rate(http_requests_total{app="webapp",version="canary"}[5m]))
```

This query shows the rate of HTTP requests served by the canary pods.

Canary Rollback Strategies

If the canary version fails, rolling back quickly is crucial.

Rolling Back to Stable Version

Option 1: Scale down canary pods

kubectl scale deployment webapp-canary—replicas=0

Option 2: Delete the canary Deployment

kubectl delete deployment webapp-canary

Option 3: Use rolling update rollback (if using a single Deployment with multiple versions)

kubectl rollout undo deployment webapp

Lessons from Real-Time Scenarios

- Always backup configuration files before applying updates.
- Keep canary Deployment minimal to limit risk.
- Use health checks and readiness probes to prevent routing traffic to faulty pods.

Practical Interview Questions on Canary Deployments

Interviewers frequently frame scenario-based questions to test your practical understanding. Here are examples:

Scenario 1: Canary Pod Crashes Immediately

Question: Your canary pod crashes after deployment. How do you debug?

Answer:

- Check pod logs using kubectl logs.
- Verify container image and tag.
- Inspect resource constraints and adjust limits.
- Use kubectl describe pod to check events.

Scenario 2: Canary Version Serving Errors to Users

Question: The canary version is running but serving errors. What steps would you take?

Answer:

- Compare canary configuration with stable version.
- Exec into the pod to inspect configuration files and environment variables.
- Analyze logs for application-level errors.
- Monitor metrics to identify spikes in failure rates.

Scenario 3: Traffic Not Reaching Canary Pods

Question: Users report they are not hitting the new version. How would you resolve?

Answer:

- Inspect service selectors and labels.
- Verify advanced routing rules in Istio or Linkerd.
- Check pod readiness probes and ensure canary pods are marked ready.

Scenario 4: Rolling Back a Faulty Canary Deployment

Question: How do you safely rollback a failing canary release?

Answer:

- Scale down or delete the canary Deployment.

- Use kubectl rollout undo if using a single Deployment with versions.
- Ensure all routing is directed to stable pods.
- Communicate rollback with the team and update monitoring dashboards.

Advanced Tips for Real-Time DevOps Interviews

- Always explain why each step is performed, not just how. Interviewers appreciate reasoning.
- Mention best practices like minimal canary replicas, automated monitoring, and gradual traffic increase.
- Highlight the importance of backup configurations and rollback readiness.
- Demonstrate knowledge of multiple routing strategies (native Kubernetes Service vs Istio/Linkerd).

Example of Gradual Traffic Increase Using Labels

Instead of routing 100% traffic to the canary, start with 10%:

kubectl apply -f canary-deployment.yaml

kubectl label pod <canary-pod> track=canary

Use advanced routing tools to gradually increase traffic based on success metrics. This ensures minimal disruption.

Real-Time Debugging Scenario

Imagine a scenario where a web application crash is reported during a canary release:

- Step 1: Inspect logs of canary pods.
- Step 2: Compare environment variables with stable pods.
- Step 3: Check resource usage and node health.
- Step 4: If issues persist, rollback canary using kubectl scale or delete Deployment.
- Step 5: Analyze root cause and update Deployment for the next attempt.

This approach demonstrates structured problem-solving—a key skill assessed in DevOps interviews.

Debugging canary deployments in Kubernetes is a critical DevOps skill. Understanding deployments, ReplicaSets, services, labels, and traffic routing is essential for successful updates. Safe monitoring, prompt rollback strategies, and structured debugging form the backbone of effective canary management.

Real-world interviews often test scenario-based knowledge rather than theoretical concepts. Candidates who can demonstrate practical steps, reasoning, and troubleshooting skills for canary deployments are highly valued.

Lab 5 — Observability & SLOs: Show Me You Can Measure Reliability

Introduction to Observability

Observability is a core principle in modern DevOps practices that enables teams to understand the internal state of a system based on external outputs. Unlike simple monitoring, which alerts teams about failures or performance issues, observability provides actionable insights that help diagnose root causes and optimize system reliability.

In real-world DevOps interviews, candidates are often asked not only to explain observability but also to demonstrate their ability to implement it in practical scenarios. Observability involves three key pillars: metrics, logs, and traces. Mastery of these pillars enables engineers to answer questions like "How do you measure system reliability?" or "How can you detect anomalies before they impact users?"

Key Components of Observability

Metrics

Metrics are quantitative measurements collected over time that describe system performance. They are usually numeric and time-series based.

- CPU utilization, memory usage, request latency, error rates, and throughput are common metrics.
- Metrics are essential for defining Service Level Objectives (SLOs) and Service Level Indicators (SLIs).

Example: Measuring HTTP request success rate using Prometheus:

```
sum(rate(http_requests_total{status=~"2.."}[5m]))
```

```
/

sum(rate(http_requests_total[5m]))
```

This query calculates the percentage of successful HTTP requests over a five-minute interval, which is critical for reliability assessment.

Logs

Logs are structured or unstructured records of events generated by applications or infrastructure components. They provide context that metrics alone cannot offer.

- Logs help in diagnosing failures, understanding unexpected behaviors, and tracing user activity.
- Centralized log management systems like Elasticsearch, Loki, or Splunk are commonly used in production environments.

Example: Using Fluentd to collect and forward logs to Elasticsearch:

```
<source>

@type tail

path /var/log/webapp/*.log

pos_file /var/log/td-agent/webapp.pos

tag webapp.logs

</source>

<match webapp.logs>

@type elasticsearch

host elasticsearch.local

port 9200
```

```
logstash_format true
</match>
```

This configuration ensures all application logs are collected, parsed, and stored in a searchable format.

Traces

Traces track the flow of a request across multiple services, revealing latency and bottlenecks in distributed systems.

- Tracing is especially important in microservices architectures where a single user request may traverse dozens of services.
- Tools like Jaeger, Zipkin, or OpenTelemetry help visualize the end-to-end request path, enabling faster root cause identification.

Example: Instrumenting a Python service with OpenTelemetry:

```
from opentelemetry import trace

from opentelemetry.exporter.jaeger.thrift import JaegerExporter

from opentelemetry.sdk.trace import TracerProvider

from opentelemetry.sdk.trace.export import BatchSpanProcessor

trace.set_tracer_provider(TracerProvider())

jaeger_exporter = JaegerExporter(agent_host_name='localhost', agent_port=6831)

trace.get_tracer_provider().add_span_processor(BatchSpanProcessor(jaeger_exporter))

tracer = trace.get_tracer(__name__)

with tracer.start_as_current_span("handle_request"):

process_request()
```

This setup allows engineers to trace the lifecycle of a request, measure latency, and detect errors in real time.

Understanding Service Level Indicators (SLIs)

Service Level Indicators are the quantitative measures that reflect a system's reliability. SLIs answer the question, "How well is this service performing from the user's perspective?"

Common SLIs

- Availability: Percentage of successful requests over total requests.
- Latency: Time taken to process requests, often measured as p95 or p99.
- Error rate: Fraction of failed requests or abnormal responses.
- Saturation: Degree to which resources like CPU, memory, or disk are used.

Example: Defining an SLI for request latency:

```
histogram_quantile(0.95,
sum(rate(http_request_duration_seconds_bucket[5m])) by (le))
```

This Prometheus query calculates the 95th percentile latency, which is commonly used to detect performance degradation.

Setting Service Level Objectives (SLOs)

SLOs define acceptable performance targets based on SLIs. They are formal statements of reliability and guide both operations and development teams.

Practical SLO Examples

- Availability SLO: “The web application must have 99.9% uptime per month.”
- Latency SLO: “95% of requests must respond within 200 milliseconds.”
- Error SLO: “Error rate must not exceed 0.5% in production traffic.”

Calculating SLO Compliance

SLO compliance is measured by comparing actual performance against defined thresholds.

Example:

If your SLI measures availability as 99.92% in a month against a 99.9% SLO:

SLO target = 99.9%

Actual = 99.92%

Compliance = (Actual / SLO target) * 100 = 100.02% (SLO met)

In DevOps interviews, being able to calculate SLO compliance and explain its operational significance is crucial.

Real-Time Observability Implementation

Step 1: Define Metrics and SLIs

Identify the most critical aspects of your system from a user’s perspective. For an e-commerce website:

- Availability: Can customers load the homepage successfully?
- Latency: Are product searches fast enough?

- Error rate: Are checkout requests failing?

Step 2: Instrument Your Application

Use libraries or exporters to collect metrics, logs, and traces. Ensure you instrument both application code and infrastructure components.

Example: Exporting system metrics using Node Exporter for Prometheus:

./node_exporter—web.listen-address=":9100"

Step 3: Set Up Alerting

Alerts should be based on SLO violations rather than raw metrics. This prevents alert fatigue and focuses attention on user-impacting issues.

Example: Prometheus alert for high error rate:

alert: HighErrorRate

expr: sum(rate(http_requests_total{status=~"5.."}[5m])) / sum(rate(http_requests_total[5m])) > 0.01

for: 5m

labels:

severity: critical

annotations:

summary: "High error rate detected in web application"

Step 4: Visualization

Dashboards help teams quickly interpret data and identify trends. Grafana is commonly used to visualize SLIs, SLO compliance, and alerts.

Example: Grafana panel for latency distribution:

- Display p50, p95, and p99 latency as line charts.

- Highlight thresholds corresponding to SLOs.
- Color-code violations for immediate visibility.

Observability in Microservices

In microservices architectures, observability becomes more challenging due to the distributed nature of services. Engineers must:

- Correlate logs across services using a unique request ID.
- Aggregate metrics at a service or endpoint level.
- Use distributed tracing to identify latency bottlenecks and errors.

Example Scenario:

A payment service depends on inventory and shipping services. If checkout latency increases:

- Check traces to see which service introduces delays.
- Inspect logs in the failing service for exceptions.
- Analyze metrics to confirm resource saturation or network latency.

This practical understanding demonstrates your ability to troubleshoot complex, real-time problems in interviews.

Case Study: Implementing Observability for a High-Traffic Web Application

Scenario: A web application serving thousands of users per minute requires observability to maintain reliability.

Step 1: Instrumentation

- Metrics: Request rates, error rates, latency, CPU/memory usage.
- Logs: Centralized using Elasticsearch for searchability.
- Traces: Distributed tracing using OpenTelemetry.

Step 2: Define SLIs and SLOs

- Availability SLI: Successful request rate.
- Latency SLI: 95th percentile response time.
- Error rate SLI: Number of failed requests per total requests.
- SLOs: 99.9% availability, p95 latency under 300ms, error rate < 1%.

Step 3: Monitor and Alert

- Prometheus collects metrics, triggers alerts when SLO thresholds are breached.
- Grafana visualizes trends and anomalies.
- Slack or PagerDuty receives alerts for critical incidents.

Step 4: Continuous Improvement

- Use SLO reports to identify recurring issues.
- Implement automation to remediate common problems (auto-scaling, circuit breakers).
- Conduct postmortems for violations to prevent recurrence.

This workflow is highly relevant to DevOps interviews because it demonstrates practical application of observability to maintain service reliability.

Advanced Concepts in Observability

Error Budgets

An error budget quantifies allowable unreliability without violating SLOs. It encourages a balance between innovation and stability.

Example:

- SLO: 99.9% availability per month.
- Allowed downtime: 0.1% → ~43 minutes per month.

Teams can use this budget to prioritize deployments and operational risk management.

Correlation Between SLIs, SLOs, and Business Impact

Observability is not just technical—it's tied to business objectives. High error rates or latency directly impact revenue and customer satisfaction.

Interviewers often ask candidates to explain how observability supports business decisions. Practical answers involve:

- Linking SLO violations to potential revenue loss.
- Showing how error budgets influence release cadence.
- Demonstrating how monitoring guides operational priorities.

Real-Time Incident Response

Observability enables proactive incident response:

- Detect anomalies before customers report issues.

- Correlate logs, metrics, and traces to identify root causes.
- Automate remediation and alert the right teams.

Example Scenario:

- Sudden spike in 500 errors detected by Prometheus alert.
- Tracing shows database connection pool exhaustion.
- Scaling database pods resolves the issue before significant user impact.

Interview-Oriented Practical Examples

Example 1: Calculating SLO Compliance

- Web application served 1,000,000 requests in a month.
- 995,000 requests were successful.
- SLO: 99.9% availability.

Actual availability = (995000 / 1000000) * 100 = 99.5%

SLO compliance = 99.5% < 99.9% → SLO violated

- Discuss how to remediate and prevent recurrence.

Example 2: Debugging Latency Spikes

- Metric: p95 latency exceeded 500ms.
- Logs: Service A is timing out when calling Service B.
- Trace: Network latency between services high during peak traffic.

Solution:

- Introduce retries or circuit breakers.
- Optimize network configuration or scale Service B.
- Monitor latency after changes to ensure SLO compliance.

Example 3: Using Error Budgets

- Monthly error budget: 43 minutes downtime.
- Incident caused 10 minutes downtime.
- Decision: Proceed with deployment, still within budget.
- Interview discussion: Explain prioritization of deployments and risk assessment using error budgets.

Observability and SLOs form the foundation for maintaining reliable, high-performance systems. Real-time DevOps interviews test candidates' ability to not only collect metrics, logs, and traces but also translate these into actionable insights, define SLIs and SLOs, and respond proactively to incidents.

Practical experience with Prometheus, Grafana, OpenTelemetry, and centralized logging tools is essential. Candidates must demonstrate structured approaches for measuring reliability, detecting anomalies, calculating SLO compliance, and using error budgets to balance innovation and stability.

By mastering observability, SLIs, SLOs, and real-time incident response, DevOps engineers can confidently showcase their ability to maintain highly reliable systems, a skill highly valued in interviews and production environments.

Lab 6 — Performance Triage: Small Load Test, Big Insights

Introduction to Performance Triage

Performance triage is a crucial skill for DevOps engineers tasked with ensuring application reliability and scalability. Unlike large-scale stress testing, which can be time-consuming and resource-intensive, small load tests allow teams to detect bottlenecks, latency issues, and resource constraints early in the development or deployment process.

In real-time DevOps interviews, candidates are often evaluated on their ability to plan, execute, and analyze performance tests efficiently. The goal is to identify high-impact insights from minimal testing, enabling teams to prevent failures in production environments. This chapter explores practical strategies for small load testing, triage techniques, and actionable insights with real-world examples.

Understanding Load Testing

Load testing is the process of subjecting a system to simulated user traffic to evaluate its performance under various conditions. While traditional load tests can be extensive, small load tests focus on lightweight, targeted testing that still provides meaningful insights.

Key Objectives of Load Testing

- Measure response times and latency
- Identify resource bottlenecks (CPU, memory, network)
- Detect configuration or deployment issues
- Evaluate system behavior under incremental load

- Provide actionable recommendations to improve reliability

In an interview scenario, explaining why small load tests are valuable—faster feedback loops, lower cost, and early detection of issues—demonstrates practical understanding beyond theory.

Planning a Small Load Test

A successful load test starts with careful planning. Key considerations include:

Define the Test Scope

- Identify critical endpoints or services. Focus on high-traffic APIs or pages with complex processing.

- Determine the type of load: steady load, spike testing, or gradual ramp-up.

- Establish test duration: small load tests usually run from a few seconds to a few minutes.

Example: For a payment service API, testing the endpoint that processes checkout requests provides maximum insight with minimal resources.

Establish Baselines

Before running tests, measure current performance metrics:

```
kubectl top pod webapp
```

```
curl -o /dev/null -s -w "%{time_total}\n" http://webapp.local/api/checkout
```

These commands provide baseline CPU, memory usage, and response time. Any deviation during testing indicates a performance issue.

Define Success Criteria

Set clear expectations for what constitutes acceptable performance:

- p95 latency under 200ms
- Error rate below 1%
- CPU utilization below 70%
- Memory usage within acceptable limits

In interviews, candidates should articulate both qualitative and quantitative success criteria to show a structured approach.

Tools for Small Load Testing

Several lightweight tools can simulate load efficiently:

Apache Benchmark (ab)

- Simple CLI tool for HTTP requests.
- Generates requests to a URL and measures latency and throughput.

Example:

ab -n 500 -c 10 http://webapp.local/api/checkout

This sends 500 requests with 10 concurrent users, providing metrics like requests per second and mean response time.

Locust

- Python-based tool for more complex scenarios.
- Allows scripting realistic user behavior.

Example Locust task:

from locust import HttpUser, task, between

```
class WebAppUser(HttpUser):

wait_time = between(1, 3)

@task

def checkout(self):

self.client.post("/api/checkout", json={"cart": [1,2,3]})
```

Run Locust in UI mode to observe request rates, failures, and latency in real time.

K6

- Lightweight, scriptable load testing tool.
- Supports JSON-based performance scripts.

Example:

```
import http from 'k6/http';

import { check } from 'k6';

export default function () {

let res = http.post('http://webapp.local/api/checkout', JSON.stringify({cart: [1,2,3]}), { headers: { 'Content-Type': 'application/json' } });

check(res, { 'status was 200': (r) => r.status === 200 });

}
```

K6 allows both CLI execution and integration with CI/CD pipelines for automated load testing.

Executing the Test

Step 1: Start Small

Begin with a minimal load to validate system behavior without overwhelming infrastructure:

```
ab -n 100 -c 5 http://webapp.local/api/checkout
```

Observe CPU, memory, network usage, and error rates. Document results for comparison during scaling.

Step 2: Incrementally Increase Load

Gradually increase concurrency or request volume to identify the threshold where performance degrades:

```
ab -n 500 -c 20 http://webapp.local/api/checkout
```

```
ab -n 1000 -c 50 http://webapp.local/api/checkout
```

Track metrics using:

```
kubectl top pods
```

```
docker stats
```

This approach allows rapid identification of bottlenecks without running a full-scale stress test.

Step 3: Monitor and Log

During testing, continuously monitor application metrics and logs:

```
kubectl logs -f webapp
```

```
kubectl top pod webapp
```

Logging helps correlate errors with load conditions, which is critical for triage.

Analyzing Results

After executing the test, analysis determines actionable insights. Key focus areas include:

Latency Trends

Plot response times versus concurrent users or requests. Look for non-linear increases, which indicate bottlenecks in application logic, database access, or network configuration.

Example Observation:

- p95 latency jumps from 150ms to 600ms at 40 concurrent users.
- Analysis may reveal database queries not properly indexed or caching misconfiguration.

Error Rates

Check for failed requests or HTTP 500 errors:

```
grep "500" webapp.log | wc -l
```

High error rates under moderate load suggest application-level issues rather than infrastructure limitations.

Resource Saturation

Examine CPU and memory usage trends:

```
kubectl top pod webapp
```

```
docker stats
```

CPU spikes without proportional latency increase may indicate inefficient computation. Memory saturation often causes pod restarts or OOM errors.

Identifying Bottlenecks

Combine latency, errors, and resource metrics to identify root causes:

- Database queries causing high latency.
- Blocking I/O operations limiting concurrency.
- Inadequate thread pool size in application configuration.
- Network saturation for high request rates.

In interviews, candidates should clearly explain how they correlate multiple data points to pinpoint issues.

Triage Techniques

Performance triage involves structured problem-solving to prioritize fixes. Effective triage includes:

Prioritize High-Impact Issues

Focus on issues affecting the user experience or system reliability:

- Latency spikes on critical endpoints
- Frequent errors causing transaction failures
- Resource exhaustion leading to service unavailability

Hypothesis-Driven Debugging

Formulate hypotheses for observed behavior and test them iteratively.

Example: Latency spikes may be due to synchronous API calls. Test by replacing synchronous calls with asynchronous execution and re-run small load tests.

Incremental Remediation

Apply targeted fixes and measure impact before large-scale changes:

- Add database indexes
- Enable caching for frequently requested data
- Adjust thread pool or connection pool sizes
- Optimize queries or service code

Document Findings

Maintaining clear documentation ensures repeatability and knowledge transfer:

- Test configuration (tool, concurrency, duration)
- Observed metrics and bottlenecks
- Remediation steps and observed improvements

Interviewers value candidates who demonstrate structured triage methodology and measurable outcomes.

Real-World Examples

Scenario 1: E-commerce Checkout Latency

- Small load test: 50 concurrent users.
- Observation: p95 latency 400ms (baseline 200ms).
- Investigation: Database queries unoptimized.
- Remediation: Added index on order table, latency reduced to 180ms.

- Insight: Small load test identified a critical performance bottleneck before production load.

Scenario 2: Microservices API

- Load test: 100 requests per second.
- Observation: One service pod crashes intermittently.
- Investigation: Memory usage exceeded limits due to unbounded cache growth.
- Remediation: Implemented LRU cache eviction policy, pod stability improved.
- Insight: Early detection prevented cascading failures under full production load.

Scenario 3: Content Delivery Application

- Load test: 200 concurrent requests for media streaming.
- Observation: Response times spiked under load.
- Investigation: Disk I/O became the limiting factor.
- Remediation: Added SSD-backed storage and tuned file caching.
- Insight: Small load test provided actionable insight into infrastructure scaling needs.

Advanced Tips for Performance Triage

Use Synthetic Metrics

- Create synthetic requests that simulate typical user workflows.

- Measure performance of the entire transaction, not just individual API calls.

Integrate Load Testing with CI/CD

- Automate small load tests on new builds.
- Monitor trends over time to detect regressions early.

Correlate Logs and Metrics

- Link logs to metrics for contextual understanding.
- Use tracing to identify slow paths in distributed systems.

Experiment with Configuration Changes

- Test different JVM, database, or web server configurations under small load.
- Identify optimal settings for production deployment.

Communicate Insights

- Prepare concise, data-backed reports.
- Highlight root cause, impact, and suggested remediation.
- Present findings in interviews as a structured case study.

Interview-Oriented Practical Questions

Question 1: Why Use Small Load Tests?

Answer: Small load tests provide early detection of bottlenecks, allow iterative fixes, require fewer resources, and give rapid feedback for high-impact insights without the overhead of full-scale stress testing.

Question 2: How Do You Identify Bottlenecks?

Answer: Correlate latency trends, error rates, and resource usage. Examine logs and traces. Test hypotheses incrementally to isolate high-impact bottlenecks.

Question 3: How Would You Approach Triage if Errors Spike During a Load Test?

Answer: Prioritize critical endpoints, analyze logs for error patterns, review metrics for resource saturation, and implement targeted fixes. Re-run small load tests to confirm improvements.

Question 4: How Can Small Load Tests Prevent Production Incidents?

Answer: By detecting latency spikes, errors, or resource bottlenecks early, small load tests provide actionable insights to prevent failures under full-scale production traffic.

Question 5: What Tools Are Most Effective for Small Load Testing in Interviews?

Answer: Apache Benchmark, Locust, and K6. Explain tool choice, demonstrate setup, test execution, and analysis for real-time troubleshooting scenarios.

Performance triage through small load tests is a practical, high-impact approach that DevOps engineers must master for both interviews and real-world operations. By focusing on targeted endpoints, measuring latency, errors, and resource utilization, and applying structured triage methods, engineers can extract actionable insights without the cost or complexity of large-scale stress tests.

In interviews, demonstrating the ability to plan, execute, analyze, and remediate issues using small load tests shows not only technical proficiency but also problem-solving skills, structured thinking, and operational awareness—qualities essential for successful DevOps professionals.

Lab 7 — Security & Compliance: Quick Audit and Fix Plan

Introduction to Security and Compliance in DevOps

Security and compliance have become integral to modern DevOps practices. With the growing complexity of cloud-native applications, microservices architectures, and continuous deployment pipelines, ensuring that systems remain secure and compliant is no longer optional—it is a necessity.

In real-time DevOps interviews, candidates are expected to demonstrate not only theoretical knowledge but also practical experience in identifying vulnerabilities, conducting audits, and implementing remediation strategies. This chapter focuses on a practical approach to quickly audit systems and develop a fix plan that mitigates risk while maintaining operational efficiency.

Understanding the DevOps Security Landscape

Security in DevOps is often referred to as DevSecOps. It integrates security practices into every stage of the software development lifecycle, ensuring that vulnerabilities are detected and mitigated early.

Key areas include:

Infrastructure Security

- Protecting cloud resources, virtual machines, containers, and orchestration systems.
- Ensuring proper configuration of networking, firewalls, and IAM roles.
- Detecting misconfigurations that could expose sensitive data.

Application Security

- Securing code, dependencies, and libraries.
- Preventing vulnerabilities like SQL injection, XSS, and mismanaged secrets.
- Performing automated code scans and dependency checks.

Compliance

- Adhering to regulatory frameworks like GDPR, HIPAA, SOC 2, or ISO 27001.
- Ensuring audit trails, logging, and monitoring for accountability.
- Implementing policies to enforce data security and operational standards.

Preparing for a Quick Security Audit

A quick audit focuses on identifying high-impact vulnerabilities efficiently. The audit process involves planning, tool selection, and scope definition.

Step 1: Define the Scope

Identify critical assets and services. Examples include:

- Production servers and Kubernetes clusters
- CI/CD pipelines and automation scripts
- Sensitive data storage and APIs
- Networking components and public endpoints

Focusing on high-value assets ensures that the audit yields actionable insights quickly.

Step 2: Establish Security Benchmarks

Use established security frameworks and best practices as a reference:

- CIS Benchmarks for cloud providers and operating systems
- NIST Cybersecurity Framework for overall risk management
- OWASP Top Ten for application vulnerabilities

In an interview scenario, candidates should explain how frameworks guide audit priorities and remediation decisions.

Step 3: Select Audit Tools

Practical audits rely on a combination of automated tools and manual checks. Examples include:

- **OpenSCAP** for compliance scanning on Linux systems
- **Kube-bench** for Kubernetes security compliance
- **Trivy** for container vulnerability scanning
- **Nmap** for network scanning
- **OWASP ZAP** for web application security testing

Conducting a Quick Security Audit

Operating System and Infrastructure Audit

- Check for outdated packages and apply security updates:

```
sudo apt update && sudo apt upgrade -y
```

- Inspect firewall rules and open ports:

```
sudo ufw status
```

```
sudo netstat -tulnp
```

- Validate user accounts and permissions:

```
cat /etc/passwd
sudo cat /etc/sudoers
```

- Ensure SSH configurations follow best practices:

```
sudo vim /etc/ssh/sshd_config
# Recommended settings: PermitRootLogin no, PasswordAuthentication no
sudo systemctl restart sshd
```

Container and Kubernetes Audit

- Run kube-bench to validate compliance against CIS benchmarks:

```
kube-bench run—targets master,node
```

- Check container images for vulnerabilities:

```
trivy image myregistry/webapp:latest
```

- Validate Kubernetes RBAC policies:

```
kubectl get clusterrolebindings
kubectl get rolebindings—all-namespaces
```

- Ensure network policies restrict pod-to-pod communication where necessary.

Application and Dependency Audit

- Scan code for common vulnerabilities:

```
npm audit

pip-audit
```

- Check for outdated dependencies and patch them:

```
npm update

pip install—upgrade <package>
```

- Validate that secrets are not stored in code repositories:

```
git grep -i "SECRET_KEY"
```

Network and Endpoint Audit

- Scan for open ports and exposed services:

```
nmap -Pn <server-ip>
```

- Ensure HTTPS is enforced and certificates are valid.
- Verify DNS configurations to prevent spoofing or misrouting.

Analyzing Audit Results

After collecting audit data, the next step is to prioritize issues for remediation. Focus on vulnerabilities that are high-risk, exploitable, and critical to business operations.

Categorize Findings

- **Critical:** Immediate risk, could lead to data breach or service disruption.
- **High:** Exploitable, may impact availability or security if unaddressed.

- **Medium:** Should be addressed in short-term planning.
- **Low:** Best practices recommendations, minimal immediate risk.

Example Findings

- Unpatched Linux kernel (critical)
- Kubernetes cluster running with default service accounts (high)
- Container image contains outdated library with known CVE (high)
- SSH root login enabled (critical)
- Unused user accounts with sudo privileges (medium)

Document Observations

- Create a clear, structured report with issue, severity, affected asset, and potential impact.
- Include references to compliance standards violated (CIS, OWASP, etc.).
- This structured reporting demonstrates interview-level professionalism.

Developing a Fix Plan

Remediation planning ensures that vulnerabilities are addressed effectively and sustainably.

Prioritize Based on Risk

- Critical and high-risk vulnerabilities first.

- Medium and low-risk vulnerabilities can be scheduled for later updates.
- Consider operational impact, downtime requirements, and dependencies.

Implement Remediation Steps

- Apply system patches:

```
sudo apt update && sudo apt upgrade -y
```

- Update and rebuild container images:

```
docker pull myregistry/webapp:latest

docker build -t myregistry/webapp:latest .
```

- Enforce RBAC policies:

```
kubectl create rolebinding restricted-access—role=view—user=developer@example.com—namespace=productior
```

- Disable insecure SSH configurations:

```
sudo vim /etc/ssh/sshd_config

PermitRootLogin no

PasswordAuthentication no

sudo systemctl restart sshd
```

- Rotate secrets and credentials, ensuring they are stored securely in a vault:

```
vault kv put secret/webapp SECRET_KEY=new_secure_key
```

Automate Compliance Checks

- Integrate security scanning into CI/CD pipelines:

trivy image myregistry/webapp:latest

kube-bench run

npm audit

- Schedule automated periodic audits to maintain continuous compliance.

Verify Remediation

- Re-run audits to confirm vulnerabilities have been addressed.
- Test system functionality to ensure fixes do not break services.
- Document evidence of remediation for compliance reporting.

Practical Interview Scenarios

Interviewers often present real-world security problems and ask candidates to triage and fix them quickly. Below are examples:

Scenario 1: Kubernetes Cluster Exposure

Question: A Kubernetes cluster is exposed to the internet with default RBAC. How would you fix this?

Answer:

- Immediately restrict access using network policies and firewalls.
- Review and enforce RBAC roles, removing default service accounts.
- Audit cluster for misconfigured pods and services.

- Re-run kube-bench to validate compliance.

Scenario 2: Vulnerable Container Images

Question: Your container image has multiple high-risk CVEs. How do you mitigate?

Answer:

- Pull the latest base image with patched vulnerabilities.
- Update dependencies and rebuild the container.
- Scan the rebuilt image using Trivy or Clair.
- Deploy the updated image using rolling updates.

Scenario 3: Exposed Secrets in Code

Question: You discover API keys hardcoded in a repository. How would you remediate?

Answer:

- Immediately rotate the exposed keys.
- Remove secrets from the code and store them in a secure vault.
- Implement pre-commit hooks to prevent secrets from being committed.
- Audit repositories to ensure no additional secrets are exposed.

Scenario 4: Unauthorized User Accounts

Question: Audit reveals several inactive accounts with admin privileges. How would you handle this?

Answer:

- Review activity logs for suspicious behavior.
- Disable inactive accounts and remove unnecessary privileges.
- Implement automated periodic account reviews.
- Document changes for compliance reporting.

Advanced Tips for Quick Security Audits

Use Pre-Built Benchmarks

- CIS Benchmarks provide actionable configurations for operating systems, containers, and cloud providers.
- Following benchmarks speeds up audit time while ensuring reliability.

Automate Reporting

- Generate audit reports in JSON, CSV, or HTML for quick review.
- Include severity levels, impacted assets, and suggested fixes.

Correlate Audit Data

- Combine logs, metrics, and audit results to identify patterns.
- Detect systemic misconfigurations, not just isolated vulnerabilities.

Integrate into DevOps Workflow

- Security checks should be part of CI/CD pipelines.
- Implement "shift-left" practices to catch vulnerabilities early in development.

Maintain Audit Evidence

- Retain reports, screenshots, and remediation logs.
- Useful for regulatory compliance and future interviews discussing real-world scenarios.

Real-World Case Study

Scenario: A cloud-native e-commerce platform needs a rapid security audit.

Step 1: Inventory Assets

- Kubernetes cluster in AWS
- Docker containers for microservices
- RDS database for customer data
- Public API endpoints

Step 2: Run Quick Audit

- Kube-bench for cluster compliance
- Trivy for container images
- OpenSCAP for Linux VMs
- Nmap for network scanning

Step 3: Analyze Findings

- Several containers using outdated libraries with known CVEs
- Default Kubernetes service accounts with cluster-admin role
- SSH root login enabled on production servers

- Missing HTTPS enforcement on API endpoints

Step 4: Develop Fix Plan

- Patch container images and rebuild
- Reconfigure Kubernetes RBAC and remove default service accounts
- Disable SSH root login
- Enforce HTTPS and update API certificates
- Rotate credentials and store in vault
- Re-run audits to validate fixes

Step 5: Outcome

- High-risk vulnerabilities mitigated
- Compliance frameworks (CIS, OWASP) satisfied
- System security posture improved without major downtime

This demonstrates a structured, interview-ready approach to auditing and remediating vulnerabilities quickly and effectively.

Security and compliance in DevOps require structured, repeatable processes that integrate audits, remediation, and continuous monitoring. Quick security audits allow teams to identify high-risk vulnerabilities efficiently, prioritize remediation, and implement sustainable fixes.

In interviews, demonstrating a practical approach to auditing, analyzing, and fixing security issues—supported by tools like Trivy, kube-bench, OpenSCAP, and automated CI/CD integration—showcases not only technical competence but also operational maturity. Real-world scenarios, structured triage, and remediation planning are key to impressing interviewers and succeeding in production environments.

100+ Real-Time Interview Questions (With BUILD-Style Model Answers)

In this chapter, you will find over one hundred real-world DevOps interview questions, organized by key domains: troubleshooting, infrastructure as code, CI/CD, Kubernetes, monitoring, security, and culture. For each question, you'll see what interviewers expect and a sample answer structured via the **BUILD** approach:

- **B** — Behavior (how you behaved or would behave)
- **U** — Understanding (your technical grasp)
- **I** — Insight (evaluation of trade-offs)
- **L** — Lessons (what you learned or improvements)
- **D** — Demonstration (code, commands, or example)

You can adapt these based on your own experience. Use the BUILD framework to make your answers structured, compelling, and memorable.

Troubleshooting

Question: A production service intermittently fails with HTTP 5xx errors. How do you approach diagnosing and resolving it?

What interviewers expect: They want to see your methodical process — log analysis, narrowing down zones, system components, rollback plan, automation of detection.

Sample BUILD answer:

B: In a prior role, our critical API service began returning HTTP 500 errors sporadically for certain customers. I was on-call and led the triage.

U: I first checked the application logs (error stack traces), the web server logs, and upstream dependencies. I correlated the timestamps of failures with system metrics (CPU, memory, network). I also pored over recent deployments, configuration changes, and database health (locks, slow queries).

I: I recognized two plausible fault domains: either the application code regression or external dependency (like database or third-party API). Rushing a rollback without confirmation could mask rather than solve the root cause. Better to pinpoint the domain first, then act.

L: I learned the importance of automated alerts tied to error rate changes, and having Canary releases to limit blast radius of a bad deploy. Also, to always preserve log context (request IDs) to trace through services.

D:

1. Use grep 'ERROR' /var/log/app/app.log | grep '500' to find error patterns.
2. Query metrics: e.g. curl -s http://prometheus/api/v1/query?query=rate(http_requests_total{status=~"5.."}[5m])
3. Compare error occurrence to deployment timestamps (from CI/CD logs).
4. If a specific code version correlates, roll back that version:kubectl rollout undo deployment api-service—to-revision=5
5. Monitor error rate post rollback.

Question: One of your microservices is memory leaking; how do you find the leak and fix it?

What interviewers expect: They expect profiling, heap dumps, root cause tracing, preventive measures (alerts, limits).

Sample BUILD answer:

B: In my last project, a Java-based service gradually consumed more memory over hours and eventually OOM'd. I was responsible for diagnosing and remedying this.

U: I used a profiler (VisualVM or YourKit) to inspect heap usage and identify objects that grew unbounded. I generated heap dumps at regular intervals (e.g. using jmap -dump). Then I analyzed object retention paths to see which references prevented GC. I also reviewed recent code changes, especially caching or in-memory collections.

I: A naive approach is to just increase memory, but that hides the root leak. Instead, we must find the retaining references and close the leak. We also must guard against new leaks by putting limits and observability.

L: I learned to use automated memory thresholds to trigger alerts, and to enforce strict code review around caches, static collections, and listeners. Also, to recreate the leak in staging early.

D:

- Command to generate heap dump:

  jmap -dump:format=b,file=heapdump.hprof <pid>

- Use Eclipse MAT to open heapdump.hprof, then inspect the Dominator Tree to find biggest retained objects.

- Suppose I found a ConcurrentHashMap with unbounded keys. I replaced it with a size-limited LRU cache (e.g. Caffeine), and added metrics to monitor map size.

Question: A build suddenly hangs during compilation in CI. How do you troubleshoot?

What interviewers expect: They want parallel build analysis, resource contention, lock dependencies, caching issues, diagnostics.

Sample BUILD answer:

B: During a sprint, one day our CI build (Gradle) suddenly stalled halfway through. I owned the investigation.

U: I checked the CI log to see where it hung (which task). I connected to the build agent (if SSH allowed) and used top, ps, or jstack to see threads. I looked for locks or expensive tasks. I also reviewed whether disk, memory, or I/O was saturated, possibly causing blocking. I checked recent dependency or plugin updates.

I: It could be due to a faulty plugin, caching misconfiguration, or deadlock in build script. Jumping to rewrite is risky; better to isolate which module or task stalls.

L: I learned to use—scan builds (like Gradle build scan) to visualize performance, and to enforce timeouts on builds to auto-fail. Also to split monolithic builds into modules.

D:

- Enable debug:

  ./gradlew build—debug

- On agent, run jstack <pid> and inspect thread dumps for deadlock.

- If plugin A's task generateDocs is stuck, disable it temporarily and rerun to confirm isolation.

Infrastructure as Code (IaC)

Question: Describe how you would design an Infrastructure as Code setup for a multi-environment cloud architecture.

What interviewers expect: They look for modularization, environment isolation, DRY (Don't Repeat Yourself), state management, versioning, testing, drift detection.

Sample BUILD answer:

B: In a project involving multiple environments (dev, staging, prod), I created a Terraform architecture that could be reused and safe across environments.

U: I organized modules per logical component (network, compute, database, IAM). Each environment had a separate workspace or state file backend (often in a shared S3 bucket + DynamoDB lock). I passed environment-specific variables. I used version control (Git) with feature branches and code review. Before applying in prod, we ran terraform plan in a staging workspace. I also used terraform fmt, terraform validate, and terraform fmt hooks.

I: The trade-off lies between too much abstraction (modules get hard to understand) vs duplication. Overly generic modules may force awkward parameters. It's critical to balance simplicity vs reusability.

L: I learned to keep modules reasonably scoped, document inputs/outputs, and maintain a shared registry of modules. I also added drift detection (e.g. terraform plan regularly) and guardrails (policy as code, e.g. Sentinel or OPA).

D:

```
# modules/network/main.tf

resource "aws_vpc" "this" { ... }

resource "aws_subnet" "public" { count = var.public_count; ... }

# modules/compute/main.tf
```

resource "aws_instance" "app" { count = var.instance_count; ... }

environments/prod/main.tf

module "network" { source = "../../modules/network" var = { public_count = 2 ... }}

module "compute" { source = "../../modules/compute" var = { instance_count = 3 ... }}

Use backend config:

terraform {

backend "s3" {

bucket = "infra-state-bucket"

key = "prod/terraform.tfstate"

dynamodb_table = "state-locks"

region = "us-east-1"

}

}

We use terraform workspace select staging etc.

Question: How do you manage secrets in IaC such that your version control doesn't leak credentials?

What interviewers expect: They expect talk of secret backends, vault integration, environment variables, encrypting state, least privilege.

Sample BUILD answer:

B: When I worked on IaC for infrastructure, I had to provision databases and API keys, but we couldn't store secrets in code.

U: I leverage secret management tools (HashiCorp Vault, AWS Secrets Manager, Azure Key Vault). In Terraform, I used providers' data source features (e.g. vault_generic_secret) to fetch secrets at runtime, not store them in code. The state file is encrypted (e.g. S3 with SSE, or Azure Storage encryption). Also, IAM policies ensure only authorized roles can read secrets.

I: One trade-off is dependency on external secret system availability; if it's down, provisioning might fail. You must deal with bootstrap secrets for the first setup. Also, fetching secrets at plan time may expose them in plan output, so set sensitive = true.

L: I learned to fetch secrets only at apply, to mark variables as sensitive, to restrict plan output, and to audit access to secret store. Also to use ephemeral secrets wherever possible.

D:

```
data "vault_generic_secret" "db" {

path = "secret/data/prod/db"

}

resource "aws_db_instance" "main" {

username = data.vault_generic_secret.db.data["username"]

password = data.vault_generic_secret.db.data["password"]

# mark as sensitive

}
```

And in Terraform:

```
variable "db_password" {

type = string

sensitive = true
```

}

State backend encryption: S3 with kms_key_id or Azure Storage with encryption.

CI/CD (Continuous Integration / Continuous Delivery)

Question: How would you build a CI/CD pipeline for a microservices architecture in the cloud?

What interviewers expect: They expect stages (build, test, deploy), isolation per service, rollback, blue-green or canary, artifact repository, integration tests, quality gates.

Sample BUILD answer:

B: In a project with multiple microservices (Git repo per service), I established CI pipelines (Jenkins, GitLab CI, GitHub Actions) and a CD pipeline (Argo CD).

U: Each service had its own pipeline: code -> compile/test -> build container image -> push to registry. Then a deployment pipeline orchestrated environment promotion (dev → staging → prod). I used feature branch previews, automated integration tests, and deployment strategies such as canary or blue/green. Rollbacks were automated. I used an artifact registry (Docker Hub, ECR) and versioned images (tags like service:v1.2.3).

I: The trade-off is complexity vs safety. Integrating all services in a single pipeline is simpler but brittle. Decoupling pipelines gives more independence but more overhead. Canary provides lower risk but needs more orchestration.

L: I learned that pipeline templates are helpful (DRY), pipeline as code is critical, and monitoring pipeline time helps optimize performance. Also, fail fast if tests fail early.

D:

```
# sample GitLab CI for service
stages:
- build
- test
- deploy
build:
stage: build
script:
- docker build -t registry.example.com/myservice:$CI_COMMIT_SHA .
- docker push registry.example.com/myservice:$CI_COMMIT_SHA
test:
stage: test
script:
- pytest tests/
deploy:
stage: deploy
script:
- helm upgrade—install myservice chart/—set image.tag=$CI_COMMIT_SHA
```

Then deploy promotion:

argocd app sync myservice-prod

Rollback automatically if health fails.

Question: How do you handle versioning and rollback of deployments?

What interviewers expect: They expect you to explain tagging, artifact immutability, rollback mechanism, database migrations, compatibility.

Sample BUILD answer:

B: On a recent team, we had to support rollback of service releases in production safely.

U: We enforced immutable artifacts (containers, binaries), tagged by commit SHA or semantic version. Each deployment is associated with a specific artifact. We maintained a history of previous versions (retaining last N images). For rollback, we executed a reverse deployment step. We also kept database migrations backward compatible where possible or used blue/green DB migration patterns.

I: The danger is database schema changes that can't be rolled back easily or cause data loss. So rolling back code is easier than rolling back schema. Another trade-off is keeping many older artifacts consumes storage.

L: The lesson was always to write backward-compatible migrations and to test rollback as part of staging drills. Also, to plan for "toggle" flags for changes that require gradual rollback.

D:

kubectl rollout history deployment myservice

kubectl rollout undo deployment myservice—to-revision=3

In pipeline:

on failure:

deploy:

script:

- HELM_PREV=$(helm history myservice –max 5 | tail -n2 | head -n1 | awk '{print $1}')

- helm rollback myservice $HELM_PREV

Kubernetes (K8s)

Question: What is a Kubernetes DaemonSet and when would you use it?

What interviewers expect: They want basic definition, use cases, trade-offs, example scenario.

Sample BUILD answer:

B: I've used DaemonSets in multiple clusters for system-level tasks like log forwarding and node instrumentation.

U: A DaemonSet ensures one (or more) replica of a pod runs on each (or selected) node. It's useful for node agents (monitoring agents, storage plugins, log shippers). When new nodes join, the DaemonSet ensures the pod is scheduled automatically.

I: The trade is that you lose scheduling flexibility for those pods—they're forced everywhere (or per selection). If the agent is heavy, it consumes resources on every node. Also, upgrades of the DaemonSet must be done carefully to avoid disruption.

L: I learned to label and taint nodes so only eligible nodes run DaemonSets, to limit resource requests for agents, and to use rolling updates.

D:

apiVersion: apps/v1

kind: DaemonSet

metadata:

```yaml
name: node-exporter
spec:
selector:
matchLabels:
app: node-exporter
template:
metadata:
labels:
app: node-exporter
spec:
containers:
- name: exporter
image: prom/node-exporter:latest
resources:
limits:
cpu: 100m
memory: 50Mi
```

Apply with kubectl apply -f daemonset.yaml.

Question: How does Kubernetes perform service discovery between pods?

What interviewers expect: They want knowledge of ClusterIP, DNS, environment variables, and limitations.

Sample BUILD answer:

B: In our microservices cluster, we used Kubernetes DNS for service discovery, and I helped troubleshoot DNS issues.

U: Kubernetes creates a Service object, which gets a stable virtual IP (ClusterIP). Pods can access other services via that IP or via DNS names (e.g. service.namespace.svc.cluster.local). Kube-DNS (CoreDNS) resolves service names. Also, Kubernetes injects environment variables (older versions) into pods pointing to services.

I: Using DNS is flexible and decoupled from IPs, but can add lookup latency or cache consistency issues. Hardcoding IPs is brittle. Another nuance is headless services, which omit ClusterIP and allow clients to resolve pod IPs directly.

L: I learned to monitor DNS performance (cache TTLs, sclerosis), to avoid too many DNS lookups, and to design clients that tolerate DNS caching. Also to use headless services for stateful sets.

D:

Service YAML:

```
apiVersion: v1

kind: Service

metadata:

name: orders

spec:

selector:

app: orders

ports:

- port: 80
```

targetPort: 8080

Access: orders.default.svc.cluster.local:80 or simply http://orders.

Question: A pod is stuck in CrashLoopBackOff. How would you debug and fix it?

What interviewers expect: They expect kubectl describe, kubectl logs, error patterns, liveness probe misconfiguration, resource limits, initialization issues.

Sample BUILD answer:

B: On one deployment, a new version of a service kept crashing repeatedly in Kubernetes, showing CrashLoopBackOff. I led the fix.

U: I used kubectl describe pod <pod> to review recent events (e.g. OOM, missing image). Then kubectl logs pod (with—previous if restarted) to read the error. I examined resource requests/limits, environment variables, and readiness/liveness probes. I also checked whether init containers were failing.

I: CrashLoopBackOff often arises from application errors, missing config, failed migrations, or health probe misconfig. Rolling back blindly may hide the root. The better trade is to gather logs and align config first.

L: I learned to always run pods in a debug mode locally first, to include fallback logging, and to limit unnecessary restarts to ease debugging. Also, set more generous initial resource limits during rollout.

D:

kubectl describe pod myapp-abc123

kubectl logs myapp-abc123

kubectl logs myapp-abc123—previous

If you find:

panic: connection refused to DB

You fix the config or secret, redeploy, and monitor.

Monitoring & Observability

Question: What key metrics and logs do you collect for a web-based application?

What interviewers expect: They want response latency, error rate, throughput, CPU/memory, infrastructure metrics, traces, logs, alerting policies.

Sample BUILD answer:

B: I built monitoring dashboards and alerts for several production services.

U: For metrics, I collected: request rate (RPS), error rate (4xx/5xx ratio), p95/p99 latency, CPU usage, memory usage, disk I/O, network throughput, garbage collection (for managed languages). For deeper insight, I used distributed tracing (e.g. Jaeger, Zipkin) to trace end-to-end request latency. For logs, I centralized structured logs with request IDs (JSON), including context (user ID, transaction ID). I also collected system logs (OS, kernel, network).

I: The trade is between collecting too much data (cost, noise) and too little (blind on issues). You must balance retention, cardinality, and usefulness. Also consider tagging and metric cardinality control.

L: I learned to alert on error rate thresholds, latency SLO breaches, CPU saturation, and anomalies (via anomaly detection). Also to build dashboards with golden signals and to conduct periodic review of alert noise.

D:

Example Prometheus query:

```
rate(http_requests_total{status="500"}[5m]) / rate(http_requests_total[5m])
> 0.01
```

Trace integration in code (for Python Flask):

```
from jaeger_client import Config
```

```
config = Config(config={}, service_name='myapp')

tracer = config.initialize_tracer()

with tracer.start_span('process_order') as span:

span.set_tag('order_id', order.id)

# business logic
```

Logs in JSON:

{"timestamp":"2025-10-12T10:00:00Z","level":"INFO","request_id":"abcd","latency_ms":1

Question: An alert is firing for high latency in one service. What steps do you take?

What interviewers expect: They expect triage flow: verify, drill down by service segment, identify root cause, act, tune alert.

Sample BUILD answer:

B: On another project, we got frequent latency alert noise. I handled the incident and then tuned alerts.

U: First, I verified the alert—is it a valid SLO breach or false positive? Then I drilled into latency percentiles (p50, p95, p99) and traced where time was spent (frontend, backend, DB, cache). I correlated with system metrics (CPU, GC pauses, network latency). I also checked recent deployments or code changes.

I: Blindly scaling the service might hide the true issue (e.g. a slow database query). It's better to isolate slow subsystems. Also, too tight latency alert thresholds generate noise.

L: I learned to build layered alerts (warning thresholds, critical thresholds), and to slice by user segments or endpoints. Also to track alert fatigue and periodically review thresholds.

D:

- Use Prometheus:

```
histogram_quantile(0.95,
sum(rate(http_request_duration_seconds_bucket[5m])) by (le, endpoint))
```

- Drill down:

top slowest endpoints:

```
sum(rate(http_request_duration_seconds_bucket[5m])) by (endpoint, le)
```

- If /checkout endpoint is slow, trace it:

trace — service A → DB → cache → external API

Tune or optimize the slowest leg.

Security

Question: How do you implement security scanning in the pipeline (SAST, DAST)?

What interviewers expect: They expect integrating static analysis, dependency scanning, dynamic scanning, fail gates, remediation loop.

Sample BUILD answer:

B: I integrated security scanning into CI for multiple services, enforcing quality gates.

U: In the build stage I ran SAST tools (e.g. SonarQube, Checkmarx) to analyze source code vulnerabilities. I also ran dependency scanning (e.g. OWASP Dependency-Check or Snyk) to detect known CVEs. In staging or QA environments, I ran DAST (e.g. OWASP ZAP, Burp) to simulate runtime vulnerabilities (XSS, SQLi). I configured thresholds so builds fail if severity > critical. Additionally, I generate reports and loop the findings back to developers.

I: The trade is build time overhead and false positives. Too strict policies may block delivery. It's important to tune severity thresholds and suppress known acceptable issues. Also, scanning dynamic workloads may require stable test data or endpoints.

L: I learned to integrate scanning early (shift left), to suppress or triage false positives, and to create developer training for remedial fixes. Also to embed scanning into PR checks.

D: In pipeline:

stage: security

script:

- sonar-scanner

- snyk test

- zap-full-scan.py -t http://staging.example.com -r zap-report.html

- if grep -q "HIGH" zap-report.html; then exit 1; fi

Results get published to build UI and emailed.

Question: How do you secure Kubernetes clusters and workloads?

What interviewers expect: They expect talk of RBAC, network policies, pod security contexts, secrets encryption, image scanning, admission controllers.

Sample BUILD answer:

B: In a recent engagement, I led a security hardening exercise for a Kubernetes cluster.

U: I used RBAC to limit permissions: least privilege roles, no cluster-admin to apps. I enabled network policies to restrict service-to-service communication. I configured pod security contexts (runAsNonRoot, readOnlyRootFilesystem). I enabled image scanning to reject vulnerable images. I enabled secrets encryption at rest (KMS) and use an external secret store like Vault. I installed admission controllers (e.g. OPA Gatekeeper, PodSecurity Admission) to enforce policies. I also banned hostPath mounts and enforced resource quotas.

I: Tight policies can break legitimate workloads, so incremental rollout is safer. Over-restricting early can lead to runtime failures. Also, security tools add overhead.

L: I learned to start with baseline policies, test in dev, monitor failures, then gradually enforce in prod. Also to audit cluster-role binding changes and to perform regular security reviews.

D: Example of network policy:

apiVersion: networking.k8s.io/v1

kind: NetworkPolicy

metadata:

name: allow-from-frontend

spec:

podSelector:

matchLabels:

role: backend

ingress:

- from:

- podSelector:

matchLabels:

role: frontend

ports:

```
- protocol: TCP
port: 80
```

Pod security context snippet:

```
securityContext:
runAsNonRoot: true
runAsUser: 1000
readOnlyRootFilesystem: true
```

Use admission:

```
apiVersion: templates.gatekeeper.sh/v1
kind: ConstraintTemplate
# define constraint to disallow privileged containers
```

Culture & Process

Question: How do you foster a DevOps culture in a team that is used to siloed dev and ops?

What interviewers expect: They expect examples of collaboration, shared ownership, blameless postmortems, automation culture, learning mindset.

Sample BUILD answer:

B: In one organization, dev and ops were separate with little overlap. I advocated and helped lead a DevOps adoption pilot.

U: I organized cross-functional squads combining devs and ops, instituted shared responsibility for metrics (uptime, deployment frequency). I introduced blameless postmortems to learn rather than blame. I ran internal knowledge sessions to teach developers about infra, and ops about application logic. I encouraged automation (CI/CD, infra as code) to reduce manual handoffs.

I: Changing culture is slow; mandating too much too early can trigger resistance. The trade is pacing vs momentum. Also, executives must support the change.

L: I learned that small wins (like automating a tedious deployment) help build trust. Metrics (lead time, MTTR) help track change. Celebrate collaboration and recognize contributions across teams.

D: We used dashboards showing deployment frequency per team, mean time to recovery, and error rates. We held monthly "DevOps retro" meetings:

- What automation did we add?
- What gaps remain?
- Action items for next month.

I also paired dev and ops engineers for on-call rotations so both sides saw each other's challenges.

Question: How do you handle conflict when an operations engineer resists a deployment change that developers request?

What interviewers expect: They expect communication, reasoning, compromise, governance, and decision framework.

Sample BUILD answer:

B: I once faced pushback from an operations engineer who felt a new deployment branching strategy introduced risk.

U: I first listened to their concerns (risk, stability, rollbacks). I assessed whether those concerns were valid (did the branching introduce extra merge complexity?). I offered to pilot the strategy in a smaller service. I proposed guardrails (canary, feature flags, rollback automation) to reduce risk. I suggested we document trade-offs, monitor metrics, and reevaluate.

I: The trade is between agility (developer velocity) and stability (ops reliability). For the long run, aligning both parties is better than one dominating. Compromise and proof by data are stronger than mandates.

L: I learned to engage stakeholders early, to present data (e.g. rollout failure rate), and to propose incremental adoption. Also, include ops in design choices rather than after the fact.

D: We set up a pilot pipeline for one microservice using the new branching model with canary deployment. We collected metrics (error rate, rollback count). After two sprints, ops saw reliability was unaffected, so they agreed to wider rollout.

More Sample Questions (Across Domains)

Below are more sample questions with condensed BUILD style outlines. You should expand with your own experience during interviews.

Troubleshooting

Question: The system clock drift is causing authentication failures in a cluster. How do you detect and fix?

- **B:** I encountered an SSO failure; tokens rejected due to timestamp mismatch.
- **U:** I checked NTP status on nodes, drift via chronyc tracking or ntpq -p.
- **I:** Trade between enforcing strict NTP sync vs tolerances.
- **L:** Use drift alerts proactively.

D:

chronyc sources

chronyc tracking

```
sudo systemctl restart chronyd
```

Question: Disk space exhaustion happens on a node, affecting pods. How do you resolve and prevent it?

- **B:** I once had a node with /var/lib/docker full.
- **U:** I identified large images or dangling volumes via docker system df, du -sh.
- **I:** Deleting images frees space but may require re-pulls.
- **L:** Use eviction thresholds and logging quotas.

D:

```
docker image prune -a

docker volume prune
```

IaC

Question: How do you test your IaC configurations before applying to prod?

B: In multiple infra projects, I insisted on tests.

U: I used terraform plan, terraform validate, unit tests (e.g. using Terratest or pytest). I sometimes spin up a sandbox environment.

I: The trade is test infra cost vs risk of faulty config.

L: Invest early in automated tests.

D:

```
// in Terratest

terraform.InitAndPlan(t, terraformOptions)
```

CI/CD

Question: How do you integrate end-to-end tests without slowing down the pipeline?

B: I faced long E2E test run times.

U: I designated quick smoke tests in the dev pipeline; heavy E2E in nightly or staging pipelines. I parallelized tests, used test shards, run in containers.

I: The trade is speed vs confidence.

L: Always prioritize fast feedback.

D:

e2e:

stage: test

script: npm run e2e——shard=1

Kubernetes

Question: Describe how you would perform a rolling update with zero downtime.

B: I led continuous deployments for services.

U: Use Deployment rollingUpdate strategy with maxUnavailable=0, maxSurge=1. Health/readiness probes ensure the pod only passes traffic when ready.

I: Faster updates may risk broken state transitions; slower is safer.

L: Always test updates in staging.

D:

spec:

strategy:

type: RollingUpdate

rollingUpdate:

maxUnavailable: 0

maxSurge: 1

Monitoring

Question: How do you detect anomalies instead of static threshold alerts?

B: On one system, threshold alerts either fired too late or too often.

U: I used anomaly detection (e.g. Prometheus' predict_linear, or ML tools) or moving baseline (e.g. deviation from rolling average). E.g. Alerts on sudden deviation rather than absolute threshold.

I: The trade is complex and noisy. Simple thresholds are easier. But anomaly detection catches weird patterns.

L: Always have fallback to threshold alerts.

D:

(http_requests_total offset 1h * 1.2) < http_requests_total

Security

Question: What is the role of a Web Application Firewall (WAF) in a DevOps pipeline?

B: I configured WAF rules as part of deployments.

U: A WAF filters malicious requests (SQLi, XSS). In pipeline, you can push rules, test against attack vectors, integrate WAF policy as code (e.g. ModSecurity rules).

I: WAF adds overhead and false positives, so testing is important.

L: Maintain rules versioning, rollback capability.

D:

```
curl -H "User-Agent: sqlmap" http://app.example.com
# ensure WAF blocks it
```

Culture & Process

Question: How do you measure DevOps maturity in a team?

B: I participated in a maturity assessment.

U: I used metrics: deployment frequency, lead time for changes, mean time to recovery (MTTR), change failure rate. Also, qualitative metrics: number of automated pipelines, test coverage, infrastructure coverage.

I: The trade is overemphasis on metrics rather than outcomes; metrics should guide not dictate.

L: Use metrics as conversation, not as punishment.

D:

We tracked monthly dashboards:

- Deploys/week
- Median lead time
- MTTR
- % of changes with rollback

Closing Thoughts on This Chapter

100+ questions may feel like a lot, but what's more important is how you **communicate** your thinking. The BUILD framework helps you deliver structured, memorable answers, and the example commands, snippets, and insights give depth. During interviews:

- Always relate to your real experiences – replace generic stories with yours.

- Use the BUILD format implicitly: state the situation, your understanding, how you reasoned, what you learned, and (if possible) show a snippet or concrete example.

- Be honest: if you haven't faced a particular scenario, describe how you'd approach it anyway.

- Don't recite definitions; focus on trade-offs and reasoning.

System Design for DevOps Interviews: Quick Blueprints Recruiters Love

Introduction to System Design in DevOps Interviews

System design is one of the most critical topics in DevOps interviews. Unlike coding or tool-specific questions, system design evaluates a candidate's ability to architect reliable, scalable, and maintainable systems. In a DevOps context, system design is not just about writing software—it's about designing operationally resilient systems, ensuring observability, scalability, security, and maintainability.

Interviewers often look for candidates who can think beyond code and focus on end-to-end system reliability, automation, deployment, and monitoring. This chapter provides practical blueprints, real-world examples, and strategies that candidates can use to answer system design questions confidently and effectively.

Understanding DevOps System Design Principles

System design for DevOps requires understanding both software architecture and operational practices. Key principles include:

Scalability

Scalability ensures that a system can handle increased load without performance degradation. There are two main approaches:

Horizontal Scaling: Adding more instances or nodes to handle traffic. For example, deploying multiple replicas of a web service behind a load balancer.

Vertical Scaling: Increasing resources like CPU, memory, or storage on existing nodes. Vertical scaling has limitations and is less flexible than horizontal scaling.

Reliability and High Availability

Reliability is the ability of a system to function correctly under predefined conditions. High availability (HA) ensures minimal downtime, usually by deploying redundant components and failover mechanisms.

Example: Deploying multiple instances of a service across different availability zones with health checks and automatic failover.

Observability and Monitoring

Observability allows teams to understand system behavior using metrics, logs, and traces. Monitoring is the active collection and alerting on these signals.

Example: Using Prometheus and Grafana to monitor CPU, memory, request latency, and error rates.

Automation and CI/CD

Automation reduces manual errors and accelerates deployments. Continuous Integration and Continuous Deployment (CI/CD) pipelines are essential for DevOps system design.

Example: Automated build, test, and deployment pipelines using Jenkins, GitHub Actions, or GitLab CI.

Security and Compliance

Security is integrated into system design, not added later. This includes secure communication, role-based access, secrets management, and adherence to compliance standards like SOC 2, ISO 27001, or HIPAA.

Example: Storing credentials in HashiCorp Vault and using TLS encryption for service-to-service communication.

Step-by-Step Approach to System Design Questions

Interviewers often expect a structured approach to system design. The following steps help demonstrate clarity and operational thinking.

Step 1: Clarify Requirements

Ask clarifying questions to understand:

- Scope and scale of the system
- User base and expected traffic
- Performance requirements (latency, throughput)
- Operational constraints (budget, compliance, uptime)

Example Questions to Ask:

- How many users are expected per day?
- What is the expected SLA for availability?
- Are there peak traffic periods to consider?

Step 2: Define Core Components

Identify the primary components of the system:

Frontend Services: Web UI, mobile app interfaces

Backend Services: APIs, business logic, microservices

Databases: Relational, NoSQL, or caching layers

Message Brokers: Kafka, RabbitMQ for asynchronous communication

Load Balancers and Gateways: Distribute traffic, handle failover

Monitoring and Logging: Observability stack for operational insight

Step 3: Design the Data Flow

Illustrate how data flows through the system. Include:

- Requests from clients to APIs
- Database queries and responses
- Asynchronous processing pipelines
- Caching layers and content delivery mechanisms

Example: User places an order on an e-commerce platform:

- Frontend sends request to API Gateway
- API Gateway routes to Order Service
- Order Service writes to Orders Database and publishes event to Kafka
- Inventory Service consumes event and updates stock
- Notification Service sends confirmation email

Step 4: Plan for Scalability

Identify components that need horizontal scaling, caching, or replication:

- Load balancers to distribute incoming traffic
- Stateless application servers for easy replication
- Database replication and sharding for high throughput
- Caching frequently accessed data in Redis or Memcached

Example Diagram:

Client → Load Balancer → Web Servers (stateless) → API Layer → DB Cluster + Cache Layer

Step 5: Ensure Reliability and High Availability

Implement HA strategies:

- Deploy services across multiple availability zones
- Set up automated failover for databases
- Use health checks and circuit breakers for service resilience
- Implement retries with exponential backoff for transient failures

Example: Kubernetes deployment with three replicas per service and PodDisruptionBudgets ensures availability during maintenance.

Step 6: Incorporate Observability

Design for observability from day one:

- Metrics: CPU, memory, request rates, error rates
- Logs: Centralized logging using ELK or Loki
- Traces: Distributed tracing for microservices using OpenTelemetry

Step 7: Integrate Security and Compliance

Design with security best practices:

- Encrypt data at rest and in transit
- Apply network segmentation and firewalls
- Use RBAC for Kubernetes and IAM for cloud resources

- Integrate automated security scanning in CI/CD pipelines

Example: Automatically scan Docker images with Trivy before deployment to production.

Step 8: Optimize for Performance

- Identify bottlenecks in database queries, service calls, or network latency
- Apply caching strategies for static content and frequent queries
- Use Content Delivery Networks (CDNs) for global users
- Implement rate limiting and throttling for API endpoints

Practical System Design Blueprints for DevOps Interviews

Blueprint 1: Scalable Web Application

Requirements:

- 100,000 daily active users
- 99.9% availability
- Real-time order processing

Design:

- Load Balancer distributes requests to stateless web servers
- API Gateway routes to microservices
- Database cluster with master-slave replication
- Redis cache for frequently accessed data

- Kafka for event-driven communication
- Prometheus + Grafana for observability
- CI/CD pipelines with automated tests and rolling deployments

Interview Tip: Explain scaling strategy, failover mechanism, and monitoring setup clearly.

Blueprint 2: Real-Time Analytics Platform

Requirements:

- Process streaming events from IoT devices
- Provide dashboards with near real-time insights
- Support millions of events per hour

Design:

- Kafka or AWS Kinesis for event ingestion
- Stream processing using Apache Flink or Spark Streaming
- NoSQL database for time-series data (Cassandra, DynamoDB)
- Web dashboard with caching layer for aggregated metrics
- Alerting system integrated with Slack or PagerDuty
- CI/CD pipeline automates deployment of processing jobs

Interview Tip: Highlight event-driven architecture, data retention strategy, and observability plan.

Blueprint 3: Multi-Region E-commerce Platform

Requirements:

- Global user base
- Low-latency response for customers worldwide
- High reliability and disaster recovery

Design:

- Multi-region deployment with load balancing across regions
- CDN for static content delivery
- Active-active database replication using cloud provider features
- Health checks and automated failover for services
- Observability stack per region with centralized dashboards
- Security measures including WAF, DDoS protection, and encrypted communication

Interview Tip: Emphasize redundancy, failover strategies, and secure design.

Common System Design Interview Questions for DevOps

Question 1: How do you design a scalable microservices architecture?

Answer:

- Decompose services based on business capabilities
- Ensure services are stateless where possible
- Use API Gateway or service mesh for routing and communication
- Implement horizontal scaling and load balancing

- Monitor service health and automate scaling decisions

Question 2: How would you ensure high availability in your system?

Answer:

- Deploy services across multiple availability zones
- Implement automated failover for databases and services
- Use health checks and load balancers to route traffic to healthy instances
- Maintain backups and disaster recovery strategies

Question 3: How do you integrate observability into system design?

Answer:

- Define metrics, logs, and traces for each service
- Use centralized monitoring and alerting tools
- Implement distributed tracing for microservices
- Set up dashboards to visualize key performance indicators and SLO compliance

Question 4: How do you handle database scaling in a high-traffic system?

Answer:

- Use read replicas for read-heavy workloads
- Shard data for horizontal scaling

- Implement caching for frequent queries
- Consider NoSQL or time-series databases for specialized workloads
- Monitor performance and adjust indices or query patterns

Question 5: How do you ensure security and compliance in your design?

Answer:

- Encrypt sensitive data at rest and in transit
- Apply RBAC and IAM policies
- Use secure CI/CD pipelines with automated scanning
- Implement logging and audit trails for compliance
- Regularly review and update configurations to meet standards

Interview Tips for System Design

Think aloud: Explain design choices clearly and justify trade-offs.

Focus on operational aspects: Include deployment, monitoring, scalability, and security, not just software logic.

Use diagrams: Simple sketches on a whiteboard or paper help illustrate architecture.

Prioritize clarity: Start with a high-level design, then drill down into components.

Address edge cases: Discuss failure scenarios and mitigation strategies.

System design in DevOps interviews tests a candidate's ability to create robust, scalable, and maintainable systems while considering operational aspects like monitoring, security, and automation. Using structured approaches, practical blueprints, and real-world examples can help candidates demonstrate their readiness for production-level challenges.

By mastering scalability, reliability, observability, security, and CI/CD integration, candidates can confidently present system designs that recruiters and interviewers find compelling and practical.

Answering Behavioral & Leadership Questions for QA/SRE Roles

Introduction to Behavioral and Leadership Interviews

Behavioral and leadership interviews are a core component of the hiring process for QA and Site Reliability Engineering (SRE) roles. While technical skills demonstrate your ability to handle system reliability, monitoring, and automation, behavioral questions assess your problem-solving approach, teamwork, communication, and leadership under pressure.

Interviewers use behavioral questions to understand how candidates handle real-world challenges, interact with teams, prioritize tasks, and make decisions during incidents. Mastering these questions is critical for QA/SRE professionals because the role involves collaboration, critical thinking, and decision-making under high-stress conditions.

This chapter provides practical strategies, structured frameworks, and real-world examples to help candidates respond effectively to behavioral and leadership interview questions in QA/SRE interviews.

Understanding the STAR Framework

One of the most effective ways to answer behavioral questions is the STAR method:

Situation: Describe the context or challenge.

Task: Explain your responsibility or objective.

Action: Detail the steps you took to resolve the issue.

Result: Highlight measurable outcomes and lessons learned.

Using STAR ensures structured, concise, and impactful answers that demonstrate problem-solving and leadership capabilities.

Example:

Situation: "Our production monitoring system was generating frequent false alerts."

Task: "I was responsible for improving alert accuracy while minimizing alert fatigue."

Action: "I reviewed alert thresholds, implemented anomaly detection, and collaborated with the DevOps team to refine metrics."

Result: "Alert accuracy improved by 70%, reducing unnecessary paging and improving incident response efficiency."

Core Behavioral Competencies for QA/SRE Roles

Problem-Solving and Critical Thinking

QA/SRE professionals encounter complex issues involving system reliability, performance degradation, or production failures. Interviewers often ask questions to assess your ability to troubleshoot and resolve issues systematically.

Example Question: "Describe a time when you identified a critical issue in production before it impacted users."

Effective Answer:

- Situation: Explain the monitoring context and initial signs of failure.
- Task: Describe your responsibility to prevent downtime.
- Action: Detail the steps, including metric analysis, log investigation, and collaboration with the development team.

- Result: Quantify the impact, e.g., "Prevented 50% potential downtime during peak hours."

Incident Management Under Pressure

SRE roles often involve being on-call and responding to incidents. Behavioral questions explore how you handle stress, prioritize tasks, and communicate during incidents.

Example Question: "Tell me about a high-pressure incident and how you handled it."

Effective Answer:

- Situation: "During a peak traffic period, our API gateway started returning 500 errors."
- Task: "I needed to restore service quickly while coordinating with the backend and network teams."
- Action: "I followed our runbook, identified the misconfiguration, applied a temporary fix, and communicated updates to stakeholders every 15 minutes."
- Result: "Service was restored in 20 minutes, and postmortem analysis led to automation that reduced similar incidents by 40%."

Collaboration and Teamwork

QA/SRE roles require collaboration with developers, product teams, and operations. Interviewers look for examples of effective teamwork and conflict resolution.

Example Question: "Describe a time you disagreed with a team member on incident prioritization."

Effective Answer:

- Situation: "During a critical outage, a developer wanted to deploy a patch immediately, but I recommended additional monitoring before applying changes."

- Task: "Ensure the system was stable while addressing the issue promptly."

- Action: "I explained the potential risks, proposed a phased deployment, and collaborated to monitor metrics during rollout."

- Result: "The system remained stable, the patch was successful, and the team appreciated the risk-mitigation approach."

Leadership and Mentoring

Even in individual contributor roles, demonstrating leadership and initiative is crucial. Leadership in QA/SRE often involves guiding teams, improving processes, and advocating for reliability practices.

Example Question: "Tell me about a time you led an improvement initiative."

Effective Answer:

- Situation: "Our alerting system was producing excessive noise, leading to delayed incident responses."

- Task: "I was tasked with improving alert quality and reliability."

- Action: "I conducted a workshop with the SRE team, analyzed alert metrics, and implemented better thresholds and escalation policies."

- Result: "Alert response times improved by 50%, and team confidence in monitoring increased significantly."

Common Behavioral Questions and Suggested Approaches

Question 1: Describe a time when you proactively identified a system issue.

Approach:

- Highlight monitoring, observability, and analysis skills.
- Show initiative in identifying and addressing potential problems before they affect users.
- Quantify outcomes whenever possible.

Question 2: Tell me about a challenging outage and how you resolved it.

Approach:

- Emphasize structured troubleshooting: isolating the root cause, mitigating immediate impact, and applying long-term fixes.
- Discuss collaboration with other teams and communication strategies.
- Include lessons learned or process improvements implemented afterward.

Question 3: How do you prioritize incidents when multiple issues occur simultaneously?

Approach:

- Explain triage methodology based on user impact, severity, and potential cascading effects.

- Mention communication with stakeholders and documentation practices.

- Example: "I prioritize Sev1 incidents affecting production traffic over internal tool failures and escalate accordingly."

Question 4: Describe a situation where you had to communicate technical information to non-technical stakeholders.

Approach:

- Show the ability to simplify complex technical issues.

- Highlight clarity, patience, and structured updates.

- Example: During a service outage, I explained the root cause, mitigation steps, and expected resolution timeline in plain language to the management team.

Question 5: Give an example of process improvement you initiated.

Approach:

- Identify inefficiencies or risks in monitoring, CI/CD pipelines, or incident management.

- Describe actions to improve efficiency, reliability, or communication.

- Emphasize measurable outcomes, e.g., reduced incident response time, improved SLA adherence.

Question 6: Tell me about a time you handled a conflict in a team.

Approach:

- Show emotional intelligence and conflict-resolution skills.
- Focus on collaboration, compromise, and constructive communication.
- Example: Mediating between a developer wanting immediate changes and the SRE team advocating for safety checks.

Leadership Skills in QA/SRE Interviews

Leadership in QA/SRE is about influence, initiative, and fostering reliability culture. Candidates should demonstrate leadership in areas such as:

Driving Reliability Initiatives

- Leading projects to improve monitoring, incident response, or automation.
- Advocating for infrastructure as code or best practices for deployment.

Example: "I led an initiative to automate rollbacks in our Kubernetes cluster, reducing recovery time from 30 minutes to under 5 minutes during critical incidents."

Mentoring and Knowledge Sharing

- Coaching junior engineers on troubleshooting, alerting, or CI/CD practices.
- Conducting workshops or documentation sessions to share operational knowledge.

Example: "I created an on-call handbook with runbooks and escalation guides, helping new engineers become productive faster."

Decision-Making in Ambiguous Situations

- Making decisions with limited information during incidents.
- Balancing speed versus risk, and demonstrating accountability.

Example: "During a partial database outage, I made the decision to failover to the standby replica while coordinating with the DB team to prevent data loss."

Leading Postmortems

- Facilitating blameless postmortems to identify systemic issues.
- Implementing process changes based on lessons learned.

Example: "After a high-severity outage, I led a postmortem session and introduced automated alerts for the previously undetected failure mode."

Practical Tips for Answering Behavioral Questions

Be Specific

- Avoid vague responses; use concrete examples from real experience.
- Include specific metrics, tools used, and results achieved.

Emphasize Impact

- Focus on the measurable impact of your actions, whether it's improved uptime, faster incident response, or reduced errors.

Show Collaboration

- Highlight teamwork, communication, and conflict-resolution skills.
- Describe how you worked with other teams or stakeholders.

Demonstrate Learning and Growth

- Show how you applied lessons learned from incidents or process improvements.
- Explain how you prevent recurrence or improve system reliability.

Keep Answers Structured

- Use the STAR method consistently.
- Ensure clarity and logical flow in responses.

Prepare for Follow-Up Questions

- Interviewers often ask technical follow-ups or ask for deeper explanations.
- Be ready to discuss tools, scripts, monitoring strategies, or decision rationales.

Example Behavioral Answer Using STAR

Question: "Tell me about a time you improved the incident response process."

- Situation: "Our team was struggling with delayed responses to high-severity alerts, causing extended downtime during peak usage."
- Task: "I was tasked with streamlining our on-call and incident response workflow."
- Action: "I implemented automated alert routing using PagerDuty, created structured runbooks for common incidents, and trained the team on prioritization."

- Result: "Response times decreased by 40%, incidents were resolved faster, and team confidence improved. Postmortems showed fewer escalations and more consistent handling of outages."

Real-World QA/SRE Scenarios for Behavioral Interviews

Scenario 1: On-Call Incident During a Holiday

Question: "Describe a time you managed an incident while on-call during a critical period."

Answer:

- Situation: "Our e-commerce platform experienced checkout failures on Black Friday."

- Task: "Ensure minimal disruption to users and restore service quickly."

- Action: "I followed the runbook, escalated to the database team, rerouted traffic to backup servers, and communicated status to stakeholders."

- Result: "Service was restored within 25 minutes, limiting revenue impact and maintaining customer trust."

Scenario 2: Automation Initiative

Question: "Give an example of automating a manual process."

Answer:

- Situation: "Our deployment process involved multiple manual steps, causing delays and human errors."

- Task: "Automate the process to improve reliability and speed."

- Action: "I implemented CI/CD pipelines using GitHub Actions and Terraform scripts to automate deployments."
- Result: "Deployment time reduced by 70%, and rollbacks became safer and faster."

Scenario 3: Handling High-Severity Incidents

Question: "Tell me about a time you dealt with a Sev1 incident."

Answer:

- Situation: "A critical microservice failed during peak usage, impacting hundreds of users."
- Task: "Restore service while identifying the root cause."
- Action: "I executed failover procedures, coordinated with development and network teams, and monitored metrics during recovery."
- Result: "Service restored within 20 minutes, and postmortem analysis led to implementing automated health checks to prevent future recurrence."

Scenario 4: Conflict Resolution in Incident Handling

Question: "Describe a time you resolved a disagreement with a team member during an incident."

Answer:

Situation: "A developer wanted to push a hotfix immediately, but I recommended testing in a staging environment first."

Task: "Balance urgency with safety."

Action: "I explained potential risks, proposed a controlled rollout, and involved the team in monitoring metrics."

Result: "Hotfix deployed safely, service remained stable, and team recognized the importance of risk assessment."

Behavioral and leadership questions in QA/SRE interviews assess your ability to handle complex incidents, communicate effectively, make informed decisions under pressure, and foster a culture of reliability and collaboration. Using structured approaches like STAR, demonstrating measurable impact, and providing real-world examples makes candidates stand out.

For QA/SRE roles, interviewers value not only technical expertise but also problem-solving, teamwork, leadership, and operational judgment. Mastery of these skills allows candidates to confidently answer behavioral questions, illustrating readiness for high-stakes, production-critical environments.

Interview Day Toolkit: One-Page Cheat Sheets & 30-Day Practice Plan

Introduction to the Interview Day Toolkit

Cracking a DevOps interview requires more than just technical knowledge—it demands strategic preparation, quick recall of concepts, and confidence under pressure. This chapter is designed to equip candidates with a complete toolkit for interview day. It focuses on **one-page cheat sheets** for rapid revision and a **30-day structured practice plan** to reinforce technical, behavioral, and problem-solving skills.

The goal of this chapter is to create a practical, actionable guide that candidates can use to maximize retention, reduce last-minute stress, and demonstrate real-time competence in interviews.

The Role of Cheat Sheets in DevOps Interviews

One-page cheat sheets serve as a condensed, high-impact reference that allows candidates to review crucial concepts in minutes. In DevOps interviews, where questions may range from CI/CD pipelines to Kubernetes troubleshooting, cheat sheets help consolidate knowledge and reinforce confidence.

Key Advantages

- Quick recall of commands, tools, and concepts
- Consolidation of best practices for monitoring, automation, and reliability
- Visual reinforcement of architectures, troubleshooting workflows, and design patterns

Suggested Format

- Divide cheat sheets into sections by topic: CI/CD, containers, cloud, monitoring, scripting, and incident management.
- Include commands, diagrams, and reminders rather than long explanations.
- Use one sheet per topic or combine multiple critical topics into a single page for rapid scanning.

Core One-Page Cheat Sheets for DevOps Interviews

Cheat Sheet 1: CI/CD Pipelines

- Essential tools: Jenkins, GitHub Actions, GitLab CI, CircleCI
- Key concepts: Build → Test → Deploy → Monitor
- Sample pipeline commands:

```
# Trigger Jenkins job

curl -X POST http://jenkins.local/job/myapp/build?token=TOKEN

# GitHub Actions run workflow

gh workflow run deploy.yml

# GitLab CI trigger

curl -X POST -F token=TOKEN -F ref=main https://gitlab.com/api/v4/projects/ID/trigger/pipeline
```

- Best practices:
  - Automate testing for unit, integration, and security
  - Enable rollback strategies in pipelines

- Integrate linting and static analysis

Cheat Sheet 2: Containers & Kubernetes

- Core commands:

```
# List pods
kubectl get pods—all-namespaces
# Describe pod
kubectl describe pod <pod-name>
# Apply manifests
kubectl apply -f deployment.yaml
# Check logs
kubectl logs -f <pod-name>
# Scale deployment
kubectl scale deployment <deployment-name>—replicas=3
```

- Kubernetes concepts:
  - Pods, Deployments, ReplicaSets, Services
  - ConfigMaps and Secrets
  - Namespaces and RBAC
- Troubleshooting checklist:
  - Pod status: Pending, CrashLoopBackOff
  - Network connectivity: Services, Endpoints

○ Resource allocation: CPU, Memory, Disk

Cheat Sheet 3: Cloud & Infrastructure as Code

- Terraform commands:

Initialize project

terraform init

Plan changes

terraform plan

Apply changes

terraform apply

Destroy infrastructure

terraform destroy

- AWS CLI quick commands:

List S3 buckets

aws s3 ls

Launch EC2 instance

aws ec2 run-instances—image-id ami-12345678—count 1—instance-type t2.micro

Check IAM users

aws iam list-users

- Best practices:

○ Version control IaC scripts

- Implement state locking for Terraform
- Use modular architecture for reusable code

Cheat Sheet 4: Monitoring & Observability

- Key metrics:
  - CPU, memory, disk, network
  - Error rates, request latency, availability
- Prometheus queries:

```
# CPU usage for all nodes
node_cpu_seconds_total
# HTTP error rate
sum(rate(http_requests_total{status=~"5.."}[5m]))
```

- Alerting guidelines:
  - Define severity levels: Sev1, Sev2, Sev3
  - Configure escalation paths
  - Include runbooks for common alerts
- Logging tools: ELK stack, Loki, Fluentd
- Tracing tools: OpenTelemetry, Jaeger

Cheat Sheet 5: Scripting & Automation

- Bash snippets:

```
# Check disk usage
```

```
df -h
# Restart service
sudo systemctl restart nginx
# Loop through files
for file in *.log; do echo $file; done
```

- Python automation:

```
import subprocess
result = subprocess.run(['kubectl', 'get', 'pods'], capture_output=True, text=True)
print(result.stdout)
```

- Automation best practices:
  - Version scripts in Git
  - Use modular, reusable code blocks
  - Include error handling and logging

Cheat Sheet 6: Incident Management & On-Call

- On-call runbook structure:
  - Identify issue → Communicate → Escalate → Mitigate → Document → Postmortem
- Quick commands for incident triage:

```
# Check system load
uptime
```

```
# Monitor active connections
netstat -tulnp
# Tail logs in real time
tail -f /var/log/syslog
```

- Communication tips:
  - Provide timely updates
  - Summarize issue and impact clearly
  - Document all actions for postmortem

30-Day DevOps Interview Practice Plan

Structured preparation over 30 days helps build both knowledge retention and confidence. This plan balances **technical practice**, **scenario-based exercises**, and **behavioral readiness**.

Week 1: Core Concepts & Command Fluency

- Focus: Core DevOps concepts, Linux commands, and version control
- Daily Practice:
  - Review one-page cheat sheets for CI/CD, containers, cloud
  - Practice common Linux commands: file operations, process monitoring, networking
  - Commit small changes to Git repositories daily
- Example Exercise: Set up a basic web app, containerize it, and deploy locally

Week 2: Containers, Kubernetes, and IaC

- Focus: Kubernetes operations and Terraform/Cloud practice
- Daily Practice:
  - Deploy a sample application to Kubernetes cluster
  - Practice scaling, rolling updates, and log troubleshooting
  - Create simple Terraform modules for cloud resources
- Example Exercise: Simulate a pod failure, troubleshoot using kubectl and resolve it

Week 3: Monitoring, Observability, and Incident Simulation

- Focus: Metrics, logging, tracing, and on-call scenarios
- Daily Practice:
  - Implement Prometheus alerts for system metrics
  - Analyze logs to detect anomalies
  - Simulate on-call incidents and follow runbooks
- Example Exercise: Introduce a CPU spike in a test pod and detect it using Prometheus

Week 4: Behavioral Preparation & Mock Interviews

- Focus: Leadership, communication, and system design questions
- Daily Practice:
  - Use STAR framework to answer behavioral questions
  - Review incident response scenarios and document postmortems

○ Conduct mock interviews with peers or mentors

• Example Exercise: Simulate a high-severity outage and practice communication with a stakeholder

Daily Routine Recommendations

• Morning: Review cheat sheets and key commands for 30 minutes

• Afternoon: Hands-on lab exercises (deploy, troubleshoot, automate) for 60–90 minutes

• Evening: Reflect on lessons learned and document improvements

Weekly Review

• Test recall of cheat sheets without referring to them

• Evaluate practical exercises: did you deploy successfully? Did incidents resolve correctly?

• Adjust next week's focus based on weak areas

Mock Interview Sessions

• Schedule at least three mock interviews before the final interview day

• Include technical, system design, and behavioral questions

• Record answers and review performance for improvement

Practical Tips for Using the Toolkit

Customize Cheat Sheets

• Tailor commands, tools, and workflows to the technologies used by the target company

- Include personal notes and shortcuts that aid memory recall

Focus on Weak Areas

- Identify knowledge gaps from previous interviews or practice sessions

- Allocate extra time for challenging topics such as Kubernetes networking or Terraform modules

Simulate Realistic Scenarios

- Combine technical exercises with behavioral practice

- Example: Deploy a service, simulate a failure, and document your incident response

Time Management During Interview Day

- Review cheat sheets for 15–20 minutes before the interview

- Keep one-page reference sheets handy for quick mental recall (not for literal use unless permitted)

- Focus on clarity, structure, and confidence when explaining concepts

Staying Calm and Confident

- Practice breathing and visualization techniques before high-stakes interviews

- Maintain structured thinking using frameworks like STAR and troubleshooting checklists

- Remember: interviewers value process and reasoning as much as correct answers

Real-World Example of Toolkit Application

Candidate: Prepares using the 30-day plan

- Week 1–2: Gains fluency in Linux commands, Git, Docker, and Terraform
- Week 3: Configures Prometheus, ELK stack, and simulates on-call incidents
- Week 4: Practices STAR responses and conducts three mock interviews

Interview Day:

- Reviews one-page cheat sheets in the morning
- Responds confidently to Kubernetes troubleshooting questions
- Demonstrates incident response simulation knowledge
- Explains system design using concise blueprints
- Communicates clearly during behavioral questions

Outcome: The structured preparation reduces anxiety, ensures recall of key concepts, and demonstrates both technical and operational competence.

The **Interview Day Toolkit**—comprising one-page cheat sheets and a 30-day practice plan—is a comprehensive approach to preparing for DevOps interviews. Cheat sheets allow rapid revision of commands, architectures, and best practices, while the 30-day plan reinforces practical skills, behavioral readiness, and problem-solving strategies.

By combining structured preparation, hands-on practice, and behavioral rehearsal, candidates can confidently tackle technical, system design, and leadership questions. This toolkit transforms scattered knowledge into actionable expertise, increasing the likelihood of success in high-stakes DevOps interviews.

Appendix A — Companion GitHub Repo & How to Show It in Interviews

In today's DevOps hiring landscape, showcasing hands-on work is as important as demonstrating theoretical knowledge. Recruiters and interviewers want to see evidence of practical skills, and one of the most effective ways to do this is through a **companion GitHub repository**.

A GitHub repository allows candidates to display real projects, infrastructure-as-code scripts, CI/CD pipelines, containerized applications, monitoring setups, and automation scripts. It provides proof that you can not only talk about DevOps concepts but also implement them in real-world scenarios.

This appendix focuses on **how to structure a GitHub repo for maximum impact**, what to include, and how to present it effectively during interviews.

Why a GitHub Repo Matters in DevOps Interviews

Recruiters often scan resumes for tools and certifications, but technical interviews dig deeper. A GitHub repo serves several purposes:

- Demonstrates practical expertise in real DevOps tools and workflows
- Provides a concrete portfolio for interviewers to explore
- Differentiates candidates from others who only list skills on a resume
- Enables discussion of decisions, trade-offs, and problem-solving approaches

For SRE, QA, or DevOps roles, a well-structured repo can highlight your ability to handle **infrastructure, automation, monitoring, and incident response** in a reproducible and organized manner.

Structuring Your Companion Repo

Repository Naming

- Choose a clear and professional name that reflects its content
- Examples: devops-interview-labs, ci-cd-automation, k8s-demo-lab

Directory Structure

A well-organized repo helps interviewers quickly navigate your work. Suggested structure:

```
devops-interview-labs/
├── README.md
├── labs/
│ ├── lab1-terraform-setup/
│ ├── lab2-kubernetes-deployment/
│ ├── lab3-ci-cd-pipeline/
├── scripts/
│ ├── deploy.sh
│ ├── monitor.sh
├── configs/
│ ├── nginx/
```

```
│ ├── prometheus/
├── docs/
│ ├── diagrams/
│ ├── design-notes.md
```

- labs/ contains all hands-on exercises and practical labs
- scripts/ includes automation or troubleshooting scripts
- configs/ holds configuration files for services, monitoring, or IaC
- docs/ provides architectural diagrams, design rationale, and notes

README File

The README.md is the most important part of your repository because it serves as a **first impression**. Include the following sections:

- Project Overview: Summarize what the repo demonstrates
- Lab Details: Brief descriptions of each lab or project
- Tools and Technologies: List tools used (Terraform, Kubernetes, Docker, Prometheus, etc.)
- How to Run: Instructions for setting up or reproducing your work
- Key Learnings: Highlight lessons learned or challenges overcome

Example snippet for README:

DevOps Interview Labs

This repository contains practical labs designed to showcase DevOps skills for interviews. It includes Terraform scripts, Kubernetes deployments, CI/CD pipelines, and monitoring setups.

Labs

- Lab 1: Infrastructure provisioning using Terraform

- Lab 2: Kubernetes deployment and scaling

- Lab 3: CI/CD pipeline with automated testing and rollback

- Lab 4: Observability setup using Prometheus and Grafana

How to Run

Clone the repo and follow the README in each lab folder. Scripts are included for automation.

Key Learnings

- Implemented IaC for reproducible environments

- Automated deployment with rollback strategy

- Set up monitoring and alerting for system reliability

What to Include in the Repo

Interviewers look for **practical relevance, clarity, and completeness**. Include:

Infrastructure-as-Code (IaC)

- Terraform or CloudFormation scripts for AWS, GCP, or Azure resources
- Modular architecture for reusable components
- Proper variable management and state handling

Example Terraform snippet:

```
resource "aws_instance" "web" {
```

ami = "ami-12345678"

instance_type = "t2.micro"

tags = {

Name = "web-server"

}

}

CI/CD Pipelines

- Jenkinsfiles, GitHub Actions workflows, or GitLab CI YAML files
- Include automated build, test, and deploy steps
- Show rollback or canary deployment strategies

Example GitHub Actions workflow snippet:

name: CI/CD Pipeline

on:

push:

branches: [main]

jobs:

build-deploy:

runs-on: ubuntu-latest

steps:

- uses: actions/checkout@v3

```
- name: Build Docker image
run: docker build -t myapp:latest .
- name: Deploy to Kubernetes
run: kubectl apply -f k8s/deployment.yaml
```

Kubernetes Deployments

- Deployment YAMLs with multiple replicas and health checks
- Services, ConfigMaps, Secrets, and scaling policies
- Monitoring sidecars or logging integration

Example snippet:

```
apiVersion: apps/v1
kind: Deployment
metadata:
name: web-app
spec:
replicas: 3
selector:
matchLabels:
app: web-app
template:
metadata:
labels:
```

```
app: web-app
spec:
containers:
- name: web
image: myapp:latest
ports:
- containerPort: 80
readinessProbe:
httpGet:
path: /health
port: 80
```

Monitoring and Observability

- Prometheus scraping configuration
- Grafana dashboards exported as JSON
- Alertmanager configurations and sample alerts

Example Prometheus scrape config snippet:

```
scrape_configs:
- job_name: 'web-app'
static_configs:
- targets: ['web-app:80']
```

Automation Scripts

- Bash or Python scripts for deployment, backup, or monitoring
- Demonstrate reproducibility and reliability in operations

Example automation snippet:

```
#!/bin/bash

kubectl rollout status deployment/web-app

if [ $? -ne 0 ]; then

echo "Deployment failed, rolling back"

kubectl rollout undo deployment/web-app

fi
```

Documentation and Diagrams

- Architecture diagrams in PNG, SVG, or PDF
- Explanations for design choices, trade-offs, and decisions
- Postmortem examples or performance tuning notes

How to Present Your GitHub Repo in Interviews

A well-prepared repo can **impress interviewers** if presented correctly. Follow these guidelines:

Prepare Talking Points

- Highlight key labs, projects, and scripts
- Emphasize the **challenges solved** and the **impact of your work**

- Include lessons learned and how it relates to production environments

Live Demo

- Optionally demonstrate your repo during the interview
- Prepare a small scenario: deploy a pod, run a script, or show CI/CD automation
- Keep it simple and rehearsed to avoid errors

Screenshots and Visuals

- If a live demo is risky, include screenshots or GIFs
- Highlight dashboards, terminal outputs, or pipeline executions

Keep it Professional

- Clean up the repo: remove unnecessary files, large binaries, or temporary scripts
- Use meaningful commit messages
- Ensure scripts run without modification on a clean environment

Emphasize Collaboration and Version Control

- Show branching strategy or pull request workflow
- Highlight commits that reflect problem-solving, collaboration, or learning

Example talking point:

"During Lab 3, I implemented a CI/CD pipeline with automated rollback. The pipeline uses GitHub Actions to build Docker images, deploy to Kubernetes, and verify readiness. The rollback mechanism ensures zero downtime in case of failure. You can see the workflow and scripts in the labs/lab3-ci-cd-pipeline folder."

Additional Tips

- Include README badges for build status or test coverage
- Use GitHub Pages or Markdown for documentation to enhance readability
- Ensure all dependencies are documented for easy replication
- Consider adding a CONTRIBUTING.md if the repo is collaborative

Real-World Example

Candidate X prepares a **DevOps Interview Lab Repo**:

- Terraform scripts to deploy AWS EC2 and S3
- Kubernetes deployment with health checks and scaling
- CI/CD pipeline using GitHub Actions with rollback
- Prometheus and Grafana setup with sample alerts
- README highlighting each lab, outcomes, and lessons learned

During the interview, the candidate:

- Explains Lab 1 and shows Terraform execution on AWS
- Opens Lab 2 and highlights Kubernetes deployment YAMLs and scaling strategy

- Discusses Lab 3 CI/CD pipeline, emphasizing rollback and testing automation
- Shows monitoring dashboards and alerts
- Uses STAR approach to explain challenges, actions, and results

Outcome: Interviewers appreciate **practical expertise, clarity, and structured thinking**, differentiating the candidate from others who only discuss concepts theoretically.

A **companion GitHub repository** is a powerful tool for DevOps interview success. It demonstrates hands-on skills, structured thinking, and problem-solving capabilities. By carefully structuring the repo, including IaC, CI/CD, Kubernetes, monitoring, automation, and documentation, candidates can present a compelling portfolio.

Equally important is **how you showcase the repo** during interviews. Prepare talking points, rehearsed demos, and visual aids, and emphasize impact and lessons learned. When done right, a GitHub repo transforms theoretical knowledge into a tangible demonstration of your DevOps proficiency.

A thoughtfully curated repository paired with confident presentation can **significantly increase your chances of success** in DevOps, QA, or SRE interviews.

Appendix B — Template Artifacts (Postmortem, Runbook, Test Plan, CI YAMLs)

In DevOps and SRE roles, demonstrating the ability to **create structured, reusable artifacts** is as critical as hands-on technical skills. Recruiters and interviewers often assess candidates not just on code or scripts but on how they document, standardize, and communicate operational processes.

This appendix provides **template artifacts** that can be referenced during interviews or even submitted as part of a candidate's portfolio. These artifacts include **postmortems, runbooks, test plans, and CI YAMLs**, all designed to reflect real-world practices. Using these templates shows interviewers that you are capable of professional, repeatable, and scalable DevOps workflows.

Importance of Template Artifacts in Interviews

Interviewers evaluate your **ability to operationalize DevOps concepts**:

- Postmortems demonstrate structured problem-solving and learning from incidents
- Runbooks showcase reproducibility and on-call readiness
- Test plans highlight your quality assurance mindset
- CI YAMLs reflect automation skills and pipeline design

These artifacts act as tangible proof of your **process orientation, reliability thinking, and collaboration skills**. They also serve as discussion points during technical and behavioral interviews.

Postmortem Template

A postmortem documents the lifecycle of an incident, identifies root causes, and proposes preventive measures. Interviewers look for structured, blameless approaches that reflect **incident ownership and continuous improvement**.

Postmortem Template Example

Incident Postmortem

Incident Title: Database Outage During Peak Traffic

Incident Date: 2025-04-03

Severity Level: Sev1

Summary

A database outage occurred during peak traffic hours, causing temporary service disruption. This postmortem outlines the timeline, impact, root cause, and mitigation steps.

Timeline

- 10:15 AM: Alert triggered by Prometheus - DB connectivity errors

- 10:17 AM: On-call SRE acknowledged the alert

- 10:20 AM: Investigated logs and identified replication lag

- 10:35 AM: Failed over to standby replica

- 10:40 AM: Service restored

Impact

- 15-minute downtime

- ~3000 user transactions failed

- Revenue impact: estimated $15,000

Root Cause

- Primary database experienced replication lag due to heavy batch jobs

- No automated failover configured for this scenario

Mitigation & Corrective Actions

- Implement automated failover for high-latency events

- Schedule batch jobs during low-traffic periods

- Update monitoring dashboards to include replication lag metrics

Lessons Learned

- Need for proactive monitoring and alerting on replication health

- Importance of regular failover drills

Owners

- On-call SRE: John Doe

- DBA: Jane Smith

- Incident Lead: Emily Clark

This template allows interviewees to **discuss a concrete scenario**, demonstrating their analytical and process-oriented approach.

Runbook Template

A runbook is a **step-by-step guide** for on-call engineers to respond to incidents. Interviewers value candidates who can **document reliable, repeatable operations**.

Runbook Template Example

Service: Web Application API

```
# Incident Type: 500 Internal Server Errors

## Symptoms

- HTTP 500 errors returned from API endpoints

- High CPU utilization on app servers

## Detection

- Alerts triggered via Prometheus: http_requests_total{status="500"} > 5/min

## Remediation Steps

1. Verify service status:

systemctl status web-app

2. Check logs:

tail -f /var/log/web-app/error.log

3. Restart service if necessary:

sudo systemctl restart web-app

4. Scale pods in Kubernetes if load-related:

kubectl scale deployment web-app—replicas=5

5. Notify stakeholders and document incident

## Verification

- Ensure HTTP 200 responses for all endpoints

- Confirm alert resolution in Prometheus
```

Using a runbook in interviews allows you to **illustrate how you handle incidents methodically**, ensuring uptime and system reliability.

Test Plan Template

A comprehensive test plan demonstrates **QA mindset and operational rigor**. It is especially relevant in DevOps interviews for roles involving continuous integration and automated testing.

Test Plan Template Example

Test Plan: Microservices Deployment

Objective

Validate that the microservices deployment is stable, functional, and meets performance standards.

Scope

- Service health

- API functionality

- Load handling

- Logging and monitoring integration

Test Types

- Unit tests for individual components

- Integration tests for service interactions

- End-to-end tests for user workflows

- Performance tests using small load simulations

Test Environment

- Kubernetes cluster with 3 worker nodes

- Database replica setup for test environment

- Monitoring via Prometheus and Grafana

Test Cases

1. Deploy service and verify pod readiness

2. Perform API calls and check response codes

3. Simulate 100 concurrent users and measure latency

4. Validate alert triggers under failure conditions

Expected Results

- All pods in Ready state

- API endpoints respond within 200ms under nominal load

- Alerts trigger within 1 minute of simulated failures

During interviews, presenting a **structured test plan** communicates attention to quality, reliability, and thoroughness.

CI YAML Template

A CI YAML file shows **automation skills** and pipeline design expertise. Recruiters look for pipelines that are **reproducible, modular, and robust**.

CI YAML Template Example

name: CI Pipeline

on:

push:

branches:

- main

jobs:

build:

```
runs-on: ubuntu-latest
steps:
- uses: actions/checkout@v3
- name: Set up Node.js
uses: actions/setup-node@v3
with:
node-version: 18
- name: Install dependencies
run: npm install
- name: Run tests
run: npm test
deploy:
needs: build
runs-on: ubuntu-latest
steps:
- name: Deploy to Kubernetes
run: kubectl apply -f k8s/deployment.yaml
- name: Verify Deployment
run: kubectl rollout status deployment/web-app
```

This template illustrates **continuous integration, automated testing, and deployment**. In interviews, you can explain why each step exists, how rollback is handled, and how monitoring is integrated.

Best Practices for Using Template Artifacts in Interviews

Keep Artifacts Simple and Readable

- Avoid overly complex templates; clarity is more impressive than verbosity

- Use consistent naming and formatting conventions

Relate Artifacts to Real Scenarios

- When discussing postmortems, runbooks, or test plans, reference real incidents or lab exercises

- Highlight **your decisions, reasoning, and impact**

Be Ready to Walk Through Artifacts

- Interviewers may ask you to explain a postmortem, runbook, or CI pipeline line by line

- Practice **explaining technical content clearly to both technical and non-technical audiences**

Include Automation and Observability

- Emphasize how templates integrate with automated workflows and monitoring tools

- Example: "This runbook automatically checks pod health and triggers alerts via Prometheus if metrics exceed thresholds"

Maintain Version Control

- Store templates in a personal GitHub repository to showcase **structured documentation**

- Commit changes with meaningful messages reflecting improvement or learning

Real-World Example of Artifact Usage in an Interview

Candidate Scenario:

- The candidate shows a **postmortem** from a lab simulating a high CPU load incident
- Walks through the **runbook**, explaining how the on-call engineer would restore service
- Shares a **test plan** validating both deployment stability and API functionality
- Presents a **CI YAML** demonstrating automated build, test, and deployment

Outcome:

- Interviewers can see **hands-on proficiency**, structured thinking, and incident management skills
- Candidate can answer follow-up questions with confidence using **documented artifacts as evidence**

Template artifacts—postmortems, runbooks, test plans, and CI YAMLs—are **essential tools for DevOps interview success.** They provide a tangible way to demonstrate:

- Operational knowledge
- Structured problem-solving
- Automation skills

- Quality assurance mindset

By creating clear, concise, and realistic templates, candidates can **show, rather than just tell**, how they approach DevOps challenges. Using these artifacts in interviews enhances credibility, highlights hands-on experience, and gives interviewers confidence in your ability to perform in real-world SRE or QA/ DevOps roles.

When prepared effectively, **template artifacts not only showcase technical expertise but also communication, organization, and leadership qualities**, which are highly valued in DevOps teams.

www.ingramcontent.com/pod-product-compliance
Lightning Source LLC
LaVergne TN
LVHW052320200926
848481LV00002B/618
* 9 7 9 8 2 3 2 0 5 9 3 7 8 *